BITTER BONDS

A Colonial Divorce Drama of the Seventeenth Century

Bitter Bonds

Leonard Blussé

translated by Diane Webb

A Colonial Divorce Drama of the Seventeenth Century

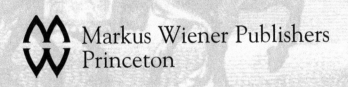

Markus Wiener Publishers
Princeton

FIFTH PRINTING, 2012

THE ENGLISH TRANSLATION WAS MADE POSSIBLE
BY A GRANT FROM THE NETHERLANDS
ORGANIZATION FOR SCIENTIFIC RESEARCH (NWO), THE HAGUE.

FOR INFORMATION WRITE TO:
MARKUS WIENER PUBLISHERS
231 NASSAU STREET, PRINCETON, NJ 08542
WWW.MARKUSWIENER.COM

BOOK DESIGN BY CHERYL MIRKIN
THIS TEXT WAS COMPOSED IN GOUDY OLD STYLE

BLUSSÉ, LEONARD, 1946–
[BITTERS BRUID. ENGLISH]
BITTER BONDS : A COLONIAL DIVORCE DRAMA
OF THE SEVENTEENTH CENTURY / LEONARD BLUSSÉ :
TRANSLATED BY DIANE WEBB.
INCLUDES BIBLIOGRAPHICAL REFERENCES.
ISBN: 978-1-55876-252-7 (HC: ALK. PAPER)
ISBN: 978-1-55876-253-4 (PBK : ALK. PAPER)
1. DUTCH—INDONESIA. 2. BITTER, JOHAN, 1638–1714.
3. NIJENROODE, CORNELIA VAN. I. WEBB, DIANE. II. TITLE.

MARKUS WIENER PUBLISHERS BOOKS ARE PRINTED IN THE
UNITED STATES OF AMERICA ON ACID-FREE PAPER,
AND MEET THE GUIDELINES FOR PERMANENCE AND DURABILITY
OF THE COMMITTEE ON PRODUCTION GUIDELINES FOR BOOK LONGEVITY
OF THE COUNCIL ON LIBRARY RESOURCES.

Contents

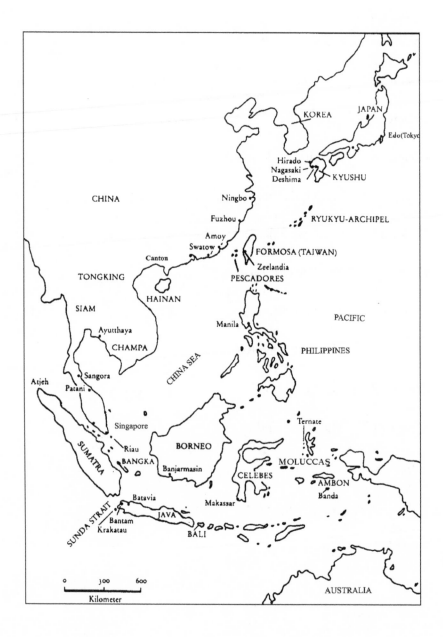

KOREA

JAPAN

Edo(Tokyo)

Hirado
Nagasaki
Deshima

KYUSHU

CHINA

Ningbo

RYUKYU-ARCHIPEL

Fuzhou

Amoy
Swatow

FORMOSA (TAIWAN)

Canton

Zeelandia

PESCADORES

TONGKING

HAINAN

SIAM

PACIFIC

Ayutthaya

Manila

CHAMPA

PHILIPPINES

CHINA SEA

Atjeh

Sangora

Patani

Ternate

Singapore

BORNEO

MOLUCCAS

Riau

SUMATRA

BANGKA

Banjarmasin

CELEBES

AMBON

Banda

Batavia

Makassar

SUNDA STRAIT

JAVA

Bantam

Krakatau

BALI

0   300   600

Kilometer

AUSTRALIA

Preface to the American Edition

In most societies, including those of the Judeo-Christian tradition, women were relegated to the subservient roles of mother, wife, sister, or daughter. Only when they overstepped the bounds of family life and became actively involved in larger social or economic issues are we likely to meet them in the public arena.

In the following tale, which was gleaned from archives in both Asia and Europe, we meet an exceptional individual who refused to be submissive, a woman whose indignation and sense of justice impelled her to fight for her rights to the bitter end. Of mixed parentage, Cornelia van Nijenrode grew up in Japan and colonial Batavia as a ward of the Dutch East India Company. Happily married to a high-ranking Company official, she was left a widow in her forties, subsequently falling into the clutches of a lawyer with five children whose wife had died on the long voyage from Holland to Java. By the time his grasping nature had become apparent, there was practically nothing she could do to keep him from robbing her of her fortune. With no family to protect her and the power of her former husband's colleagues on the wane, she was left to her own devices.

The original version of this tale was a ninety-page-long study on the legal status of women in colonial society, with the telling title *Butterfly or Mantis? The Life and Times of Cornelia van Nijenroode*. Because of its multicultural background, the essay was translated into three Asian languages. In Japanese it even appeared as a beautifully edited monograph. Nevertheless, these very literal translations—with excessively detailed footnotes referring to practically inaccessible sources and obscure academic issues—prompted me to rewrite the story for a much wider readership. Upon its appearance in 1998, *Bitter's Bruid* (Mr. Bitters Bride) received mixed reviews. Although it was awarded the Golden Owl, a prestigious prize for Dutch non-fiction, it elicited differing responses from reviewers and readers alike. In some reviews the story was discussed as if it were a work of fiction: I was even criticized for not including more dialogue between the main characters. In answer to this I can only say that, as a historian, I did not feel free to fill the book with dialogue, however much the limited nature of the historical sources tempted me to pad them out.

Other readers blamed me for not siding more openly with the heroine against her overbearing husband. Some women even sent personal letters recounting lengthy court battles of their own, which had convinced them that divorce proceedings had not changed much over the past three hundred years. Indeed, the protracted legal battle between Cornelia and her husband prompted the German publisher to give the book the rather unoriginal but nonetheless revealing title *Der Rosenkrieg* (The War of the Roses). Japanese readers, for their part, read their own cultural values into the story, recognizing in Cornelia a "woman warrior" valiantly fighting for a lost cause. A documentary made for Japanese television even suggested that the heroine had committed ritual suicide to preserve her honor and save her inheritance for her grandchildren. The reactions I occasionally receive from Indonesian readers show that, while they feel less affinity with the main characters, they take the story to be a condemnation of the colonial past.

For a writer it is interesting to see how every reader interprets a historical tale within the context of his or her own culture. After I had pieced together the available evidence in Holland, Indonesia, and Japan, and had started to record this story of trench warfare between husband and wife, I became increasingly fascinated by the various ways in which the colonial community reacted to this public drama. To the reader who recognizes an element of classical tragedy in this struggle between two strong characters I should like to point out the old adage "The past is a foreign country; they do things differently there."

It was only recently, while writing *Retour Amoy*—the biography of an elderly Chinese Indonesian woman now living in China—that I discovered how exhilarating it is for the biographer of a contemporary person not only to enter into discussion with his subject but also to be reproached by her for misinterpreting the material. All this is impossible, however, when the person one is writing about lived more than three hundred years ago. In such a case the most one can do is empathize.

Long ago the townspeople of Hirado, Cornelia's birthplace in Japan, erected a small pagoda to her memory. Though I regret not having succeeded in tracking down her final resting place, I hope I have comforted her wandering soul by telling this tale of her tenacious quest for justice. She may not be the kind of role model the correspondents of the History World Web are looking for, but her vicissitudes certainly shed light on the position of women in the past.

CHAPTER ONE

Otemba

Prologue

The spring of 1712 had been stormy and cold, with snow falling as late as April. But in spite of the unpredictable weather, nature seemed to take its course, for in May the orchards outside the town walls of Wijk bij Duurstede burst into blossom. As happened every spring, the local residents rediscovered the pleasures of an evening walk past the town gate and out into the surrounding countryside. Strolling along the dike, they could take in a lovely view of the Lower Rhine, studded with the sails of barges. The town in the background—embraced by its high, grassy ramparts—floated like a wreath on a sea of blossoms.

Johan Bitter, the elderly burgomaster of Wijk bij Duurstede, had retreated to his apple orchard in the polder behind the Bemmel Dike outside the town gate. The past week had seen a great deal of commotion in his townhouse on Oeverstraat, with the servants busily preparing for the arrival from Batavia of his daughter Bartha, her husband, and her eldest son Constantijn. The news that the fleet had just arrived must have spread across the country like wildfire. Johan Bitter was expecting them to arrive at any moment.

To escape all the hustle and bustle, he had left the house after the midday meal and strolled over to his orchard. He was obviously quite tired, for instead of taking a catnap he fell into a deep sleep. The maid, worried because her master had not come home for supper, walked over to the orchard with a pot of broth and found him asleep in his garden house, snoring away on the ebony sofa he had brought from Batavia. When he asked if there had been any news of the travelers, the maid shook her head and handed him a letter from his son Arnolt that had been delivered to the house that afternoon.

"Then they won't be arriving today," muttered the old man and decided to stay a while longer before returning to town.

Johan Bitter went outside to sit on a bench and sip his broth in the late afternoon sun. After filling his pipe he turned to Arnolt's letter. He broke the seal on the envelope and unfolded the letter, his eyes falling on the familiar handwriting of his only son. The salutation—"My dear father"—was followed by a list of all the letters Arnolt had received from him since the previous year. There had been five altogether. "Let me think. Five? Yes, that's right," mumbled Bitter to himself. "What else does he have to say? Just the usual news about people coming and going." Bitter skimmed the letter quickly. "Is cousin Van Wiert in Cochin ever going to amount to anything? And how are things with cousin Van Meekeren? Oh, here Arnolt writes about him":

I am pleased to see that cousin Van Meekeren is now behaving better than he used to. I feel there is hope for him, though it will be a long time before he is in a position to help his mother. The Indies are not the land of plenty that one imagines. Promotion is a slow process, and the less fortunate never see any profits whatsoever.

"This letter is all about the things I sent. I'll look at it more closely at home," mumbled Johan Bitter as he glanced at the list of goods that followed. "Wait a minute, here he talks about the foolish plans of his sister Eva and her husband Hendrick, who are thinking of going to the Indies to marry off their daughters. I forgot I'd written to him about that." Bitter put his glasses more firmly on his nose and resumed his reading.

To tell the truth, if my necessary expenses did not exceed my usual income, and if I were lucky enough to have such an important position as brother Both [a burgomaster], I would never think of leaving my fatherland, especially if I weighed 220 pounds and my wife 180. Such fat people are not fit for the Indies; I feel this myself, I who have never even weighed 180. To undertake the voyage for the good of their daughters is also foolish, because here they are just as much a source of embarrassment as in Holland. Everyone must do as he sees fit, though. As the saying goes, the wearer knows where the shoe pinches.[1]

"My feelings exactly," grumbled Bitter, "but it's a shame you had to put it so bluntly, son, because now I can't let Eva and Hendrick read your letter." Stopping for a minute to think about what he had just read, he laid the epistle on his knees and looked around vacantly. His attention was soon drawn to the couples walking arm in arm, surrounded by their romping children. The large windmills on the ramparts in the background, which seemed to guard the town like mighty watchmen, reminded him of the two gigantic statues of fierce-looking generals that flanked the entrance to the klenteng, the Chinese temple just outside the town walls of his beloved Batavia.

The memories prompted by Arnolt's letter, the paragons of conjugal bliss parading past—it all set him thinking. He, too, had once had a taste of wedded bliss, but it had not been granted him a second time. On the contrary, his second marriage had been a disaster. But had that been his fault? At least one good thing had come of it: Arnolt, who had been in the East for ten years now, seemed to have learned from his father's mistakes. The old man picked up the letter and started to read again:

I would like to move back to Holland in about three years, by which time I should be in a position to live in Amsterdam in style. Last September I entered the forty-eighth year of my life, so that I shall be about fifty-one at the time of my repatriation.

After careful consideration, I now see that it would be inadvisable to tie myself down to a wife here, risking my peace of mind by putting myself at the mercy of a woman's fickle moods. Marriage would throw me into life's maelstrom again, especially if I were to marry a woman of child-bearing age, as I certainly would if I decided to marry at all.

Then, however, I might never decide to undertake the journey to my beloved fatherland, and I would be in danger of having to spend the rest of my life here, slaving away till the end of my days. It is no longer possible to marry for money in Batavia. A man must be prudent and contribute everything he can to the support of his family.[2]

"Good lad," mumbled the old man. "I understand. In the East children are a millstone around your neck. That's why my dear Bartha sent her two boys to live with me." But what had Arnolt said at the end of his letter? Were there no more rich matches to be made in Batavia? And that remark about being prudent and supporting one's family: had he meant that as a sly dig?

"Marriage—what was it Hugo Grotius said about it?" he wondered, continuing to mull over the problem. "Lawful marriage is the union of a man and a woman to a common life, bringing with it the lawful use of each other's body."

Use of each other's body? Yes, the Romans called marriage matrimonium and with good reason. You marry a woman to make her a mater, a mother. Marriage therefore exists for the purpose of procreation. "Nubilis and nubilus," he murmured softly. "Strange how those words are so similar. One means marriageable, the other overcast or melancholy. Is that a coincidence? Perhaps not. After all, brides traditionally wear veils during the wedding ceremony."

He knocked the ashes out of his pipe and looked around with obvious pleasure at the beautiful blossoms in his apple orchard before reading on . . .

Colonial Customs and Japanese Traditions

In the early colonial period of the Dutch East Indies, nearly four hundred years ago—the period in which this story takes place—European men who pursued a career in the service of the Dutch East India Company often elected not to marry, owing to the difficulties frequently encountered by those who did. Company men went overseas at an early age to make money, lots of it, and they sought consolation in liquor and the caresses of a native housekeeper. If they survived their stint in the tropics, where life was twice as grueling but also twice as lucrative as life in Holland, without ruining their health (the liver in particular), they often returned home—still only middle-aged—and retired to a life of leisure.

Sometimes they even tried to make up for lost time by marrying a

View of Hirado, looking out to sea. The Dutch trade factory was situated on the left-hand side of the entrance to the harbor. (Shiba Kokan, Sayu Nikki, 1788)

much younger woman. This remained the normal state of affairs until the end of the nineteenth century, when colonial life was completely changed by the opening of the Suez Canal and the resulting influx of great numbers of white women.

The situation was somewhat different for the merchants of the remotest settlement of them all, the Dutch trade factory on Hirado, a picturesque island in the south of Japan. Between 1609 and 1860 the average Company employee—referred to as "John Company"—lived and worked under quite exceptional circumstances in the Empire of the Rising Sun. Initially, Dutch merchants were free to conduct trade on Hirado. The daily life of the Dutch in those parts largely followed the pattern set by the Chinese sailors who had been coming there for years. If a junk or an East Indiaman put in at the bay of Hirado, dropping anchor in the midst of the southern monsoon, then the crew knew that a hot summer was in store. The sailors could do nothing but bide their time until the monsoon season was over and they could once again set sail with a northern breeze. If they had enough money in their pockets (and they usually did on this leg of their journey), the men inevitably sought female companionship. When a sailor climbed on board again in the autumn, seen off by his girlfriend of three months, the sadness of parting quickly gave way to a feeling of excitement at the thought of all the females waiting for him at the next port: the Siamese girls of Patani, the jet-black women of Coromandel, and the slave girls of Bali who were sold for a song in Batavia. Life also returned to normal for the Japanese lovelies who stayed behind in Hirado. The girls went back to their parents' homes, where they probably spent the winter looking forward to the arrival of the ships the following spring. One or two trading seasons were enough to provide them with the dowries they needed to secure respectable Japanese husbands. The path taken by these women, whom the Japanese called *karayuki-san*—meaning those who go abroad, or in this case, fraternize with foreigners—was not unacceptable in old Japan.

Four hundred years ago, some of the Dutchmen stationed in Hirado enjoyed life there so much that they stayed behind to move in with a Japanese woman and start a family. In 1640, however, this option came to an abrupt end. Several years previously, the supreme ruler of Japan, the shogun Tokugawa Iemitsu, had issued a series of decrees—the so-called *kaikin*, or "maritime prohibition laws"—forbidding his subjects to go abroad. Foreigners were henceforth refused entry into Japanese harbors: only the Dutch and the Chinese were still welcome, and then only under the observance of strict conditions. The Company warehouses in Hirado were subsequently razed to the ground by order of the shogunate, and the Dutch merchants were forced to relocate to the fan-shaped island of Deshima in the bay of Nagasaki, where a completely new life was in store for them.

The dozen or so Dutch merchants who spent the winter on Deshima were housed in Japanese-style wooden houses, together with their Asian slave-servants. A sentry posted on the only bridge connecting the island of Deshima with the city of Nagasaki monitored all in- and outgoing traffic. *Metsuke*, or Japanese spies, kept tabs on what happened on the island itself. Only the Dutch head merchant (*oranda kapitan*) and a few members of his staff were allowed to leave Deshima every spring to undertake the long journey to the shogun's palace in Edo (present-day Tokyo), where they paid tribute, on behalf of the Dutch East India Company, to the secular ruler of Japan.

When the ships from Batavia appeared in the bay of Nagasaki in August, all hands gathered on Deshima to watch them unload their precious cargo: spices from Banda and Ternate, silk and cotton from India, pewter and sugar from Batavia, worsted from Holland, as well as such exotic animals as ostriches, Persian horses, and greyhounds. The merchandise was inspected and then stored in warehouses or put in stables on the island until the viewing days and auctions in September. Over the course of several weeks everything was sold, at which time the loading of the return cargo began, around the beginning of October. First to be put on board were the bars of silver; later on, when Japan's reserves of silver had shrunk, it was copper, porcelain, lacquer ware, and camphor. When the crew of the East Indiaman weighed anchor sometime before "the twentieth day of the ninth lunar month"—to the sound of drums, sea shanties, and the deafening roar of a cannon salute—and the ship was towed out of the bay by dozens of sampans, the small garrison of those staying behind waved goodbye to their sea-faring friends and then went into hibernation, so to speak. The only jobs remaining were to monitor the supplies, check the accounts, and keep the journal up to date. Once these activities had been seen to, the boredom of the daily routine inevitably set in.

Drinking, eating, playing billiards, reading, making music, and fur-tively conducting a bit of private business on the side: all this helped to kill time, but it was not enough. What John Company missed most on that small island, surrounded by the bustling harbor town of Nagasaki with its colorful night life, was female companionship. Dutch women were not permitted to enter Japan, for a settlement of white people on Yamato soil was something the proud ruler would not tolerate.

Fortunately for the foreigners, a way was found to make life on Deshima more bearable. Shortly after the factory was moved to the island in 1641, the Dutch chief factor—the head of the Dutch trade factory—went to the governor of Nagasaki to ask for his advice. He had been racking his brains trying to find a solution to the problem of total celibacy presently confronting himself and his men. Every evening, he stated in his petition, all the Japanese personnel left the post. The sen-tries, the informers, everyone—including the servants—went to the mainland and did not return to the island until the following morning. "Who is supposed to serve us tea in the evening if there aren't any women on the island?" was the question he put to his host.

This cunning query was met by the Japanese governor of the city with understanding. Henceforth women of easy virtue from Nagasaki's

Maruyama quarter were permitted to keep the Dutchmen company at night, and so almost every evening the Lady Butterflies tripped across the bridge in their rustling silk kimonos to do what was expected of them. But however docile and self-effacing these Japanese women seemed to be in Western eyes, John Company soon got to know another side of their personality. These girls had a lot of experience, not only in cheering up their clients but also in keeping them in line. And it must be admitted that the heavily perspiring, bored-looking Dutchmen were a curious breed. Not only did they wash themselves infrequently, but they consumed huge quantities of salted beef, causing them to stink from every pore, at least by Japanese standards. The fact that they also drank too much brandy did nothing to help their breath either. Moreover, when they were drunk and didn't get their way, they were in the habit of shouting incomprehensible obscenities in their graceless, guttural language. The geishas had their own solution to this problem: they did what was expected of them as courtesans, but there was a time to come and a time to go. And so every night they returned to the city, thereby preserving their elusiveness. When a courtesan skipped back across the bridge in the early hours of the morning, it was often to the accompaniment of a hoarse male voice, calling after her, "Untamable is what you are, untamable." The Dutch for "untamable"—*ontembaar*—lives on in Japanese to this day: *otemba*. A female who goes her own way—whether an unruly child or an adolescent girl with a will of her own—is still called *otemba* in Nagasaki.

The Dutch are fond of pointing to a long tradition of female assertiveness in their own society. Because their collective memory goes back no further than the Batavians—the early tribes who settled in the Rhine delta as Roman allies—the writer Tacitus is habitually quoted as the foremost authority on the Dutch national character. Around the beginning of the Christian era, the Roman author expressed astonishment at the prominent position occupied by women in the Germanic tribes. In later centuries, however, when the Low Countries had been pacified by Roman troops, there was little left of this brazen independence. According to Roman-Dutch law, women were completely subordinate to men. A woman was not considered "competent in law to act on her own behalf, and the man was named husband and guardian of his wife."[3]

Nowadays we can scarcely imagine how far-reaching the consequences of this inequality before the law must have been, not only for the woman herself but also for the laws pertaining to property ownership in Holland's materialistic society. The husband had full disposition of his wife's property, for the law stated that a woman did not have the right to manage her own assets without the permission of a male guardian, usually her father, husband, or other male relative.

Whether this was inspired by Roman law or was simply viewed as one of the responsibilities of the head of the family, the jurist Hugo Grotius, writing in the early seventeenth century, saw it as a clear-cut situation: "In this country the wife's possessions are largely subject to the guardianship of the husband."[4] In legal matters the husband spoke for his wife. He could dispose of and mortgage her property as he saw fit, "also those assets which she does not hold jointly with him, without requiring her consent to do so." The letter of the law may have said as much, but did people act accordingly? Even Hugo Grotius did not attempt to conceal his amazement at the extent of the man's legal powers in the Netherlands. This raises a number of questions.

Did all women accept this legal incapacity without a struggle, simply because they didn't know any better? Or did they sometimes lay down the law, like the courtesans of Deshima? Alas, such headstrong behavior was all but impossible—their hands were legally tied—so women usually resigned themselves to their fate, as it says in the Bible: "Unto the woman he said, I will greatly multiply thy sorrow and thy conception; in sorrow thou shalt bring forth children; and thy desire shall be to thy husband, and he shall rule over thee" (Genesis 3:16).

How did the God-fearing Dutch react in centuries past to a woman with a sharp tongue who had the nerve to cry out for justice when she caught her husband squandering her fortune? As Hugo Grotius clearly states, divorce was well-nigh impossible. As long as the husband did not commit adultery, there was little—legally speaking—that could be said against him. Obviously, in such cases every effort was made to reconcile squabbling spouses, especially as they were considered to have been rendered inseparable by both the law and their nuptial vows. In practice, most cases in which the woman considered herself the injured party were settled out of court. She would have been told in no uncertain terms not to contest her husband's God-given rights; indeed, she did not have the legal capacity to do so. In such cases the rebellious spouse would also be kept in line by social control exerted by the family, the church, and the community. Only when things got completely out of hand and the husband beat his wife "or otherwise treated her cruelly" was a judge called into action. Then, if their troubles persisted, a legal separation was permitted, with the understanding that continued attempts be made to reconcile the couple.

Was there a more depressing prospect for the father of a bride-to-be than a son-in-law likely to make off with the dowry? Problems of this kind were apparently so frequent that it was not the couple-to-be but rather their parents who sat down with a notary to draw up a kind of prenuptial agreement, the so-called marriage settlement. If, however, the wife suspected she was in danger of being left a pauper through her husband's misappropriation of her assets, she could demand a legal division of their estate, which meant that theoretically her husband could no longer exercise control over her property. Such settlements did not in fact affect the judicial process: everything and everybody still held fast to the fundamental inequality of the sexes. For this reason the history of Dutch matrimonial law is a half-told tale. The female voices have been stifled, for men have always taken charge of their wives' possessions—for better or for worse—and there was virtually nothing the wife could do about it.

Nevertheless, once in a while a Cassandra appeared on the scene whose voice rang out loud and clear, so clearly, in fact, that no one knew how to handle the situation. Tragically, such women always fought a losing battle, claiming rights they were not entitled to in the male-dominated society in which they lived. Their complaints were duly recorded but seldom heard, and their case files were relegated to dusty archives.

Clio, the muse of history, occasionally takes pity on her devotees. Several years ago I stumbled across some stray documents in the archives of the Dutch East India Company regarding a woman of Dutch-Japanese descent whose marital problems were the talk of Batavia for many years, when, as a widow, she fell into the clutches of a greedy, tight-fisted second husband. After delving further into the archives of the Supreme Court of Holland and Zeeland, I came across the records of her divorce proceedings, which dragged on for fifteen years. The wronged wife, offering heroic resistance to what amounted to the theft of her property, succeeded in exposing all the legal and human shortcomings of society at that time. But before we become acquainted with the heroine of this story, let us pay a visit to Batavia, the colonial city where she lived more than three hundred years ago.

The Batavian Widow

If there was one thing that visitors to old Batavia always agreed upon, it was that family connections and money determined the course of daily life in the city that housed the Asian headquarters of the Dutch East India Company. David van Lennep, the impoverished scion of a patrician family who had traveled to the East at the end of the eighteenth century in hopes of making his fortune, understood at once how

A meeting of the Heren XVII. (Detail of a print reproduced in "Gouvernement de la Compagnie des Indes orientales," *Atlas van Stolk*, Rotterdam)

things stood. Seemingly shocked, he wrote the following to one of his relatives in Holland:

> Scraping together money in every possible way is the basic law here in Batavia, so much so that it is openly admitted. Anyone who says otherwise is taken for a fool. Listen to the logic of their arguments. "The journey here is long and dangerous, the climate unhealthy and grueling. These sacrifices and dangers must be compensated for. A man cannot make his fortune without the good will of those more powerful than he. It would be foolish to behave more considerately than others and to display more discretion in one's actions, thereby failing in the great aim that brought us here." And practice is fully in keeping with this loathsome theory![5]

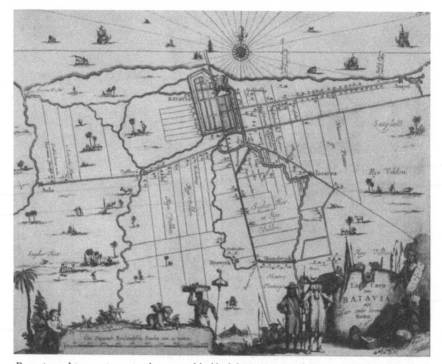

Batavia and its environs in the second half of the seventeenth century. (Johan Nieuhof, *Zee- en Lant-Reize, door verscheide Gewesten van Oost-Indien*, Amsterdam 1682)

Just how Van Lennep intended to strike it rich becomes clear when we examine more closely the peculiarities of Batavian society. Apart from the occasional midwife, all the employees of the Dutch East India Company were men. When Jan Pieterszoon Coen founded Batavia in 1619, he wrote to the collective directorate of the Company, the Heren XVII (Gentlemen Seventeen), that he would like a couple of shiploads of "marriageable young women": four to five hundred Dutch girls from ten to twelve years of age, accompanied by a few older ones. "Without women the male sex cannot exist," he wrote. Otherwise how could the population grow? It was as though he had ordered a shipment of wombs. A contemporary tells us that the garrison of Batavia welcomed the first shipload of "young women" on board the East Indiaman 't

Wapen van Hoorn as they would a shipment of "stewed pears." Coen had his own opinion of these ladies, and he recorded it in his next letter to the Heren XVII: "It was an ungodly bunch who made a lot of trouble, and some of them even behaved worse than the stupidest of beasts, causing horror and outrage among many of the natives, who, not seeing any other, better women, thought that the entire Dutch nation must be just as godless, unreasonable, and ill-mannered as these creatures."[6] In the following years as well, according to Coen's successors, the supply of "livestock" from Holland remained woefully inadequate, both in quality and quan-tity.

At some point in the 1630s, the Heren XVII resolved to try a different method. They decided that henceforth, "following the example of the Portuguese," the colony in the Indies must be supplied with women from Asian stock. With an eye to cultivating a loyal citizenry, the colonial authorities now began to encourage marriages with native women. "The Indies are too large for us to possess alone, and this country is too small to send out the great numbers of people required by colonization," wrote the Heren XVII with suspicious modesty. It was obviously time to take a different tack. Resolutions were passed that discouraged as much as possible the sending of Dutch girls—"they do not produce any enduring fruit"—and encouraged the influx of Asian women "with whom one can produce clever, robust children who survive."[7] Batavia then issued a summons for marriageable girls to be sent from various trading posts in Asia, though the Portuguese-speaking slave girls from the Coromandel and Malabar coasts in southern India were apparently in the greatest demand. After arriving in Batavia, these immature little things were sent to school to learn the true—Dutch Reformed—faith and to acquire good manners before marrying. With the help of school and catechism these girls were given a speed course in becoming mothers of the elite—condescendingly referred to by the Dutch back home as the *tropenadel,* or the "aristocracy of the tropics"—growing in due time into typical Batavian matrons who spoke Portuguese at home and broken Dutch in public.

There was, however, a hitch in this new policy: when a Company employee who had married "a native black woman" wanted to return to the Netherlands at the end of his term of service, his wife and children were not allowed to accompany him. The adoption of Portuguese marriage practices was therefore a clever ploy to keep Company personnel in the Indies, thereby guaranteeing continuity in the Dutch colonial presence in the East.

It is hardly surprising that John Company was more likely to take a concubine than a wife. Should he wish to return to Holland, he could buy off his obligations to his mistress and any children he had produced with her. However, the church authorities in Batavia refused to sanction concubinage—no matter how well the system seemed to function—because it was at odds with the concept of Christian matrimony. Baptism and marriage were the reins by which the church held the urban population in check, for those who were not baptized could not marry, and those who were not married could not have their children baptized.

More tormenting than the constraints cooked up by the Dutch Reformed Church, however, were the murderous tropical climate and John Company's own unhealthy lifestyle. Three out of four who sailed to the East never again set eyes on the dune-lined coast of Holland. Some remained in the Indies by choice, but most of them fell prey in the prime of their lives to one of the numerous epidemics afflicting Batavia and other colonial settlements.

With the exception of the freeburghers, who were self-employed, Dutch men in the East were generally employees of the Company. Though their monthly wages were modest, the rake-off in colonial trade was considerable, which meant that they usually enjoyed a large supplementary income, the so-called emoluments. Positions such as head cashier at Batavia Castle, boss of the Company's shipyard on the island of Onrust facing Batavia, or chief factor of the island of Deshima in far-off Japan were posts highly sought after by the profiteers among the personnel.

Nicolaus de Graaff, for example, ship's surgeon and chronicler of Company life in Batavia, related a scene he had witnessed at Batavia harbor in the 1670s. Returning from Deshima, chief factor Hendrick Cansius boasted to the Governor-General, Cornelis Speelman (himself an unrivaled speculator), that during the previous trading season in Japan more money had changed hands in private trade (which was strictly forbidden) than in Company business. Speelman, clearly embarrassed by such a public display of bragging, said "Hold your tongue, man. No one asked about your private business," and turned his back on Cansius. "But," De Graaff could not resist adding, "when the private merchandise was unloaded, the ship rose three and a half feet!"[8]

Another notorious profiteer was the official in charge of the island of Onrust, Willem van Hogendorp, the father—amazingly enough—of the incorruptible Gijsbert Karel van Hogendorp, the author of the Dutch Constitution. When Willem van Hogendorp set sail for the Netherlands at the end of his career in the Indies, one of the people waving goodbye to his ship is said to have mumbled, "If God is indeed almighty he will surely prevent that scoundrel and his cache of plundered possessions from reaching home." And so it came to pass. Several weeks later Van Hogendorp's ship and everyone on board went down in the Indian Ocean.

Normally Company employees stipulated in their wills that their relatives in the Dutch Republic could collect any wages still to be paid by the Company cashier. The money and possessions they had acquired illegally in the Indies were usually left to their surviving relatives and friends there. It is hardly surprising, therefore, that many a Batavian widow found she had been left a considerable sum of money by her late husband. Nor were women who had gone through three or four husbands an exception in Batavia. And so a strange situation arose in which young, ambitious bachelors like David van Lennep considered a mature widow to be a much more desirable match than a young girl. Rather than reflecting "praise of older women," this attitude clearly illustrates the realization that these women were, quite simply, a good investment.

Women in Batavia by no means confined themselves to playing a passive role in the accumulation of wealth. They entered into all sorts of business transactions with the full knowledge of their husbands, who, as Company employees, were forbidden to get involved in such affairs. The Company turned a blind eye, however, to the private trade carried on by its employees in Japan, if only because it was impossible to check up on what those stationed at such far-off trading posts were doing. If the rules had been strictly enforced, the Company would have found itself in a bind: without the enticement of considerable financial gain, no one would willingly spend a year on the isolated island of Deshima. In Batavia, on the other hand, the regulations restricting private trade—the "spillover trade"—were strictly observed, which meant that an enterprising wife could come in quite handy. These "respectable ladies" were directly involved in local commerce: they hired out slaves, bought and sold real estate, and acted as moneylenders to the Chinese merchants. Not surprisingly, the seventeenth-century traveler and diamond merchant Jean Baptiste Tavernier attributed a great deal of influence to Batavia's matriarchs: "They are able, for the most part, to exploit their husbands' sympathy and affection so effectively that they often cause their husbands to become enmeshed in illicit dealings, the women themselves becoming involved in wrongdoings by the authority of their husbands."[9]

To Remarry or Not to Remarry

A Batavian matron who had been born and bred in the East and was used to managing a household of slaves generally led a less strenuous life than her Dutch counterpart. Although this is difficult to prove on the basis of statistical evidence, we may assume that women in Batavia generally lived longer than their husbands. Only during and shortly after childbirth were they at greater risk of dying. From a study of the careers of the "qualified personnel"—the Company's higher-ranking employees in Asia, whose appointments were due not only to merit but also to their tough constitutions—it appears that senior officials whose wives died almost always remarried the wife of a deceased colleague.

Well-to-do women in the Indies generally remarried several times. Contemporary sources confirm the important role played in Batavian society by the widows of highly placed Company employees. In the eighteenth and nineteenth centuries, nearly all members of the well-to-do middle class were descended from the offspring of the second or third marriages of senior Company officials. The wives of those second and third marriages were widows who had either grown up in the Indies or lived there a good many years. Moreover, at the end of the seventeenth century it became common for Company employees to own large estates in the hinterland, and so the Batavian elite finally put down roots.

These observations raise a number of questions. Was the mature, well-to-do Batavian widow aware of the trump card she was holding when a man began courting her? Did her financial standing and her business acumen prompt her to make certain demands on prospective husbands? Did these "merry widows" make conscious use of marriage to an established Company official or a young, rising star as a means of climbing higher up the social ladder? Or did they passively endure the advances of these young cavaliers, doomed to fall prey to men who were only after their fortune? In 1820, John Crawfurd, who had held various posts in the Indies during the time of the English interim government, had this to say about it: "As soon as a woman becomes a widow, and the body of her husband is interred, which is generally done the day after his decease, if she be but rich, she has immediately a number of suitors.

A certain lady, who lost her husband while I was at Batavia, had, in the fourth week of her widowhood, a fourth lover, and, at the end of three months, she married again, and would have done it sooner, if the laws had allowed of it."[10]

We could of course view this anecdote about life in Batavia from a purely romantic perspective, but what legal protection did a woman who owned property actually have? Did the legal system allow an unattached widow to go her merry way and continue her business activities without the protection of a husband? And if she remarried, could she carry on doing business without her husband's express permission? Certainly not, for Dutch law applied to her as well. In theory her husband administered her property, and only if he gave his express permission for her to act as a "public tradeswoman"—which, as we have seen, could be to his advantage—did she enjoy any freedom of action.

Now that we have become acquainted with the wealthy widow as a prominent personality in Batavian society and have asked ourselves in passing what the women themselves thought of their position, let us try to get to the bottom of the suitors' true motives. The further outpourings of the previously mentioned David van Lennep are very telling in this respect. As he admitted in his letters, he had left for the East in order to redress the mistakes of his youth by regaining his lost fortune and paying back his debts. Van Lennep made it look as though after his arrival in the Indies—and remember that in Batavia he was at a safe remove from his creditors in Holland—he was so shocked at the local profiteering that he no longer sought a lucrative position in the government, being satisfied instead with his appointment to the Court of Justice. However, it soon became apparent that he had no intention of abandoning his plans to get rich as fast as possible.

This wolf in sheep's clothing had in fact set his sights on a widow who was rumored to be worth 800,000 guilders. In a letter to friends in Holland, he wrote about the prospect of his future wife's fortune, which would automatically come under his guardianship as soon as the marriage was solemnized. In time, he thought, he would be able to pay back his debts, which amounted to 270,000 guilders (several million dollars in today's money).

Yet Van Lennep was forced to admit, to his great regret, that it would not be possible to pay back such a large sum all at once without selling a great many assets at a loss and without embittering his future wife by handling her fortune in that way: in short, without losing her trust. But he closed noble-mindedly with the words, "I am prepared to sacrifice myself in the attainment of this goal, but it would be wrong to sacrifice one's fellow men, and worse still to betray or ruin a woman who is willing to share her glorious destiny with me!"

Luckily it never came to this. The lady in question made extensive inquiries into Van Lennep's previous conduct, and when the sins of his youth came to light, she dropped him at once. This course of action shows that at least one Batavian widow knew what she was worth. But in order to see what could happen when a Batavian dowager was trapped into marrying, discovering too late that the bonds of matrimony had tied her to a scoundrel who was only after her money, we must turn to one of the longest-running colonial lawsuits of the seventeenth century: Van Nijenroode versus Bitter. But first let's get acquainted with the heroine of our story, of whom two portraits exist, one silent and one very vocal indeed.

CHAPTER TWO

Period Piece

V isitors to the spacious gallery devoted to the Dutch East India
Company in the Rijksmuseum in Amsterdam seem a bit lost at
first, overwhelmed by the great number of ship models and paintings all
around them. Their attention is soon drawn, however, to a painting
near the middle of the room: a large portrait of the members of an "aris-
tocratic" Batavian family, the prosperous Company merchant Pieter

Pieter Cnoll with wife and daughters. (Painting by Jacob Jansz. Coeman, Rijksmuseum
Amsterdam)

Cnoll and his Asian-looking wife and daughters. This striking portrait may be viewed from at least three perspectives: those of the art connoisseur, the historian, or simply the casual viewer.

The first thing a connoisseur of art would notice is that the portraitist, Jacob Janszoon Coeman, painted in the style of his contemporary fellow townsman Thomas de Keyser, as witnessed by his choice of palette and rendering of figures. Like De Keyser, he portrayed the sitters with relatively large heads and small hands. The composition of the picture, painted in 1664, is also reminiscent of the splendid family portraits that Anthony van Dyck had produced some thirty years earlier of the luxury-loving harbor magnates in the Italian city of Genoa. Head merchant Pieter Cnoll, his wife Cornelia, and their two daughters Catharina and Hester are portrayed here on the terrace of their shady summer house outside Batavia. In the shadows behind them are two dark-skinned servants. Dimly visible in the left background are two East Indiamen, the proud sailing ships of the Dutch East India Company to which the family owed its prosperity. Their portrait leaves no room for doubt: this wealthy and influential merchant's family did not feel weighed down by an "embarrassment of riches."

Little is known about the painter Coeman. According to Company archives, he left for the Indies in 1663 in the capacity of *ziekentrooster*, or "comforter of the sick." This appointment may well have been a pretext to provide Coeman the portrait painter with new patrons. "Comforters of the sick" assisted the fleet's chaplain in his pastoral work on board ship. They were not allowed to preach but functioned instead as lay readers, reciting texts from the Bible or the catechism. After their arrival in the Indies, these reasonably literate men were frequently put to work as schoolmasters in the more remote settlements. Coeman, however, was permitted to stay in Batavia and set to work at once painting portraits of the local Company elite. Not much more can be gleaned from archival documents concerning his stay in the Indies. In the minutes of meetings of the Batavia church council his name occurs regularly as an active member of the congregation until his death was recorded on 9 April 1676.

A casual viewer, particularly a Dutch one, looking at the Cnoll family portrait may be reminded of fading family snapshots taken in the Dutch East Indies at the turn of the twentieth century. The typical East Indian attributes strike one immediately. Notice, for example, the opulence on display: the dazzling silk gowns, the pearls, diadems, and fans of the Three Graces, or the gold buttons and beautiful sash worn by Pieter Cnoll, first head merchant of Batavia Castle, portrayed here in full dress uniform as captain of the civic guard. Mother Cornelia's showpiece, the skillfully worked ivory

A miniature screen with the portrait of a young woman, which was sent to Japan from Batavia. Tradition has it that the woman represented is Cornelia. (Kanko shiryokan, Hirado)

betel box in the lap of her daughter Catharina, is truly an eye-catcher. Behind the family stand two barefoot household slaves. The female slave, wearing a *sarong kebaya*, holds a basket of tropical fruit in her arms. The male slave, nonchalantly posing with his doublet half unbuttoned and the banner of the civic guard slung over his left shoulder, slyly steals a piece of fruit from her basket. He may take the liberty of doing so, for he is his master's favorite.

The historian, who knows the eventual fate of those portrayed, will look at the painting in a completely different light, seeing it as a way of underscoring the important position held by the family in the public life of the city. In addition, this "snapshot" of a happy couple also reveals something about their personalities. The head merchant of Batavia Castle, reputed to be the wealthiest man in the city, had this family portrait painted shortly before his sudden and unexpected death. At his side, coming somewhat to the fore, is his wife, Cornelia van Nijenroode. She was the youngest daughter of an influential official—his career went back to the Company's inception—and his Japanese concubine, Surishia of Hirado.

Cornelia, with her Asian appearance and slender figure, looks directly at the viewer. Her proud pose leaves no doubt as to who ruled the roost. Behind her, portrayed here in his younger years as a mischievous slave, is Untung. Later, as the robber chief Surapati, he and his band of runaway slaves would become the terror of the Batavian countryside, and he would even end his days ruling his own kingdom in eastern Java.

In short, a silent portrait like this reveals a lot more than would appear at first glance. What a stroke of luck that Cnoll commissioned Coeman to paint this family portrait, for otherwise we would have no likeness of the heroine of this story, whom we see here as a proud mistress whose frail frame conceals her strong-willed, intractable character, with which we shall soon become acquainted.

There are, however, two more extant "portraits" of Cornelia that present another picture of her: the image of a young lady, cleverly cut out of a small wooden screen, and two of her letters, from which she emerges as a devoted Japanese daughter, a paragon of filial piety. To see these relics we must travel half way around the world to the place of her birth in Japan.

Filial Piety

Looking today at the sleepy little island of Hirado, situated off the northwest coast of the island of Kyushu, one can well imagine that in the Middle Ages it was home to a notorious band of pirates. Approaching ships could be easily observed from the tower of the white castle situated at the entrance to the narrow harbor.

At the beginning of the seventeenth century, when Tokugawa Ieyasu brought the whole of Japan under his rule, the robber barons of Hirado decided to turn over a new leaf; saying farewell to the pirate's life, they soon emerged as the protectors of peaceful overseas trade. The island even blossomed briefly as an entrepôt of goods from China, Southeast Asia, and Europe, and a great many Chinese, English, and Dutch ships put in at its harbor. The English merchants did not last a decade in Hirado, whereas the Dutch stayed for thirty years. Sailing into the harbor, one saw the Dutch trade factory, in use from 1609 to 1641, on the right-hand shore.

A well—near the gray, stone steps descending to the landing stage of the barges—and a paved path known as the "Dutch path" (*oranda ishidatami*), which climbs up the hill to a lookout on top, are all that is left to remind us of the Dutch presence of yesteryear.

With a bit of imagination the present-day visitor can still form an impression of what Hirado was like in those days. The imposing country house of the Matsuura family—a complex of dark wooden buildings, their blue roof tiles gleaming in the sunlight—lies, half-concealed, high up in the wooded hills above the port. This mansion, a long wooden pavilion once condescendingly described by John Company as a "bad piece of carpentry covered with thin tiles," now houses the family museum of the Matsuuras. Skillfully embroidered silk gowns, lacquer ware and porcelain, gleaming swords, and other weapons are exhibited against a backdrop of scrolls depicting Chinese junks and Dutch East Indiamen. Japan's illustrious past is on display in this museum, where

The *koyoto* or "piety pagoda" on the grounds of the Zuiun temple in Hirado, commemorating Cornelia's devotion to her mother. (Photo Pao)

chirping girls lead groups of tourists in slippers across the creaking floorboards.

This is not all, however. Halfway down the "Dutch path" is an unassuming little building that houses a historical collection devoted to the daily life of the subjects of the Matsuuras, the ordinary folk of this small harbor town. It is little more than a cabinet of curiosities, a motley collection of heirlooms and dusty, moth-eaten curiosa. The central show-case displays some objects once owned by a courtesan from the olden days, Surishia. These personal belongings, the focal point of a local cult, feature two letters sent from faraway Batavia in 1663 and 1671 by Surishia's daughter. Although she had been taken from her mother in Hirado when still a little girl, this devoted daughter had never forgotten her "mommy" (*okachan*) and had done everything she could to send her love and support from the Dutch East Indies.

These are the letters written by Cornelia van Nijenroode to her mother. Local tradition has it that the young lady depicted on the miniature wooden screen exhibited next to the letters is a portrait of Cornelia. The letters, written in Japanese on rice paper, made a deep impression on the population of Hirado three hundred years ago. They were found to be so exemplary that a stone pagoda was erected in honor of this devoted daughter, a paragon of filial piety (*oya koko*), and the pagoda has remained the focus of her cult to the present day.

Two pictures of Cornelia van Nijenroode have therefore been preserved: in the Far East a miniature cutout on a screen and two letters written in Japanese in which she speaks as a loving daughter; in the West the family portrait in Amsterdam's Rijksmuseum in which she is portrayed as a respectable member of the Dutch East India Company establishment. Genealogical spadework in the Company archives has made it possible to weld these two very different pictures into the portrait of one remarkable woman.

The Father, John Company

Cornelia's father, Cornelis van Nijenroode of Delft, was a member of the same generation as Jan Pieterszoon Coen, founder of the Dutch empire in Asia. Both men died in their boots, far from home, after a long career with the Dutch East India Company. But whereas Coen left for Rome as a boy of twelve to learn Italian bookkeeping, young Van Nijenroode was trained as a gem dealer. When he joined the same fleet as Coen in 1607, he was employed as a diamond expert. Once abroad, Van Nijenroode began applying his keen intellect to more than just the assessment of precious stones. This was not always appreciated, however, because he was burdened with a demanding and faultfinding nature, qualities we will encounter later in his daughter.

No one was safe from the sharp tongue of merchant Van Nijenroode. Captain Willem Ysbrandtszoon Bontekoe of Hoorn, author of a well-known travelogue,[1] experienced it firsthand and even complained of it in a querulous letter to his fellow townsman and patron, the above-mentioned Governor-General Jan Pieterszoon Coen. Van Nijenroode served as senior merchant and squadron commander aboard Captain Bontekoe's ship during the notorious China expedition of 1622, which started with an unsuccessful Dutch attack on Portuguese-held Macao. This attempt to open up China to Dutch trade eventually deteriorated into little more than a series of sporadic raids, in which women and children were abducted from the Chinese coast with the aim of increasing the Chinese population of the recently founded city of Batavia. During these raids, senior merchant Van Nijenroode poured verbal abuse on the good captain, calling him "a sloppy skipper and a haughty man," simply because he dared to disagree with him. The ship was obviously too small for two captains.

Van Nijenroode was also regularly at loggerheads with his immediate superior, Admiral Cornelis Reijersen. The cocksure merchant always knew everything better, and from the very beginning he had objected to the plan (devised by Jan Pieterszoon Coen) of using force to make the Chinese open up their coastal harbors to Dutch ships, reminding his superiors of the invasions of Korea carried out twenty-five years earlier by the notorious Japanese general Toyotomi Hideyoshi. The latter's attempts to invade China via Korea with an army of 140,000 samurai had met with total failure. Now, with only a dozen ships and a thousand men at its disposal, how did the Dutch Company imagine it could impose its will on a powerful empire? The very thought of it filled Van Nijenroode with horror, and he did not hesitate to say so. To Admiral Reijersen's credit, he recognized Van Nijenroode's qualities despite his critical views and even looked upon this straight-talking man as his successor.

Fate, however, would have it otherwise. When Van Nijenroode put in at the Japanese island of Hirado to stock up on provisions for the fleet, he was confronted with the sudden death of Leonard Camps, head of the local trade factory. On the basis of his rank and seniority, Van Nijenroode was chosen on 21 November 1623 by the factory's council to be its new chief factor. He was relieved to be able to stay behind in Hirado, a place more to his liking than the swaying deck of a ship. The feudal lord of Hirado was especially pleased with the new appointment: as difficult as he had been for his Dutch colleagues, Van Nijenroode was polite and obliging toward his Japanese hosts. His years in the service of the East India Company had certainly taught him how to behave in Asia.

After arriving in the Indies in 1607 on board the ship *Delft*, Van Nijenroode had spent twelve years at various places in the kingdom of Siam: first two years at court in the former capital Ayutthaya, followed by five years in the southern harbor towns of Sangora and Patani, where he led a life of leisure surrounded by servile concubines. Finally, he spent another five years in Ayutthaya, this time as chief factor. The diplomatic experience he acquired at the opulent Siamese court, rife with intrigue, stood him in good stead in Japan, where foreign merchants were treated no less haughtily, for the fact is that Van Nijenroode, through no fault of his own, found himself in an extremely sticky situation in Hirado.

When the China adventure ended in failure—the Dutch had built a fort on the Pescadores Islands, directly across from the Chinese coast, but were driven away by imperial troops in the summer of 1624—they decided to establish a trading post on the slightly more distant island of Formosa. The sailors had barely begun to erect fortifications at the entrance to the bay of Tayouan (near the present-day city of Tainan) when the newly appointed Dutch governor of Formosa began to seek opportunities to bully the Japanese merchants who had long been trading there with the Chinese. Hearing about this from returning Japanese traders in Hirado, Van Nijenroode again warned the High Government in Batavia that the Company should not treat Chinese and Japanese traders as high-handedly in their home waters as it was used to doing in the Indonesian archipelago. Unfortunately, this advice fell on deaf ears.

Three years later the governor of Formosa, the arrogant Fleming Pieter Nuyts, was so openly contemptuous of the Japanese traders that they retaliated: they requested an audience, overpowered his guards, and held both him and his little son hostage in their own home. Nuyts was freed after lengthy negotiations, but the terms of his release were very humiliating. Nuyts's son was even taken to Japan to be held as surety for his father's good behavior. And that was not all, for when the Japanese returned to Nagasaki and reported what had happened to them in Formosa, the shogunal authorities also decided to get even. All Company ships in Japan were unrigged and their crews put behind bars. The shogun even announced a trade embargo until he had obtained satisfaction for the affront.

Despite these stormy events, the lord of Hirado left his friend Van Nijenroode and his personnel undisturbed at the trade factory. Even though the Dutch warehouses were put under seal, the chief factor and his staff were allowed to come and go as they liked. Shortly before the embargo went into effect, Van Nijenroode had in fact sent his letter of resignation to the Governor-General in Batavia because his contract had expired, but since no ships were allowed to leave the harbor he made the sensible decision to hang on. Instead of worrying about Company affairs, he set his sights on a more relaxed life with two local beauties at his side: Tokeshio and Surishia, each of whom eventually bore him a daughter. In the summer of 1631, however, Van Nijenroode was partially paralyzed by a stroke. Had it perhaps been brought on by his inner agitation at the desperate position into which the Company had maneuvered itself? Or were two mistresses too much of a good thing for a middle-aged man who had spent so many years in the tropics?

At any rate, the next summer, when the scapegoat Pieter Nuyts was ordered by the High Government in Batavia to go to Japan and justify his behavior, he found upon his arrival in Hirado a degenerate old man. "Nijenroode is so weakened (I shall refrain from naming the illness to blame for this) that he has not been out of his room for a whole year. Moreover, he has been struck by the hand of God, so that he can neither feel nor use one side of his body," reported Nuyts. That autumn Van Nijenroode felt his strength declining to such an extent that he decided it was time to give farewell presents to those most dear to him. His two darlings, Hester and her slightly younger half-sister Cornelia, received a "large gold chain" and a Japanese *koban*, a heavy gold coin. His assistant Coenraad Salomonszoon, his Japanese servant Sansabro, and the two concubines were also given something, "for long years of service to His Worship."

Owing in part to Nuyts's appearance in Japan—where the local authorities promptly put him under house arrest—the embargo was finally lifted. The Dutch sailors who were still alive were released from prison and began carrying out urgently needed repairs on the ships that had been rotting in the harbor for four years. A spark of hope was even kindled in the exhausted invalid Van Nijenroode; perhaps he would be able to go home after all. He divided the goods he no longer needed among his Japanese friends, and on 19 January 1633 he had the rest of his possessions packed in thirty-nine trunks and crates and brought on board the *Heusden*, which lay in the harbor ready to set sail for Batavia. It was a colorful collection of bric-a-brac, Malay daggers, silverware,

silk, satin, lacquer ware, porcelain, silk kimonos, diamonds—altogether more than three hundred items. Twelve days later a long box was
added to these: Cornelis van Nijenroode's coffin. He had died shortly
before he was due to be carried on board, "broken and emaciated, rid-
dled with disease and misery."

From his will it became evident that Van Nijenroode had not had
sufficient time to put his affairs in order. He left a conventional will
providing for the needs of his next of kin: he bequeathed 2,000 guilders
to two nieces in Holland, and left one of his nephews "all his weapons,
without exception." Tokeshio, the mother of Hester, received 300 taels
of Japanese silver ingots, and Surishia, Cornelia's mother, received 200
taels, more than enough for dowries that would secure them Japanese
husbands. To each of his daughters he bequeathed "500 taels and gold
chains" and "any other small ornaments to be found in [his] furniture."
Silver ewers, beakers, candlesticks "and their snuffers" went to friends
in Batavia. All this was in addition to the goods that had already been
packed up and the outstanding loans that still had to be collected.[2]

Only after the *Heusden* had arrived at Batavia did the High Government discover the extent of the fortune Van Nijenroode had amassed
during his ten-year stay in Japan. The general conclusion was that all
those things could only have been collected "by means of dishonest
dealings or by conducting illegal and private business." The entire
estate was therefore confiscated by order of the Court of Justice and
sold at public auction. The proceeds from this sale, no less than 23,000
guilders, went straight into the Company coffers, because, according to
the Batavian authorities, the deceased merchant had "sinned against
the ordinance forbidding private trade." As we saw earlier, the authorities took a more lenient attitude to private trade in later years, when
the Dutch factory was moved to the more isolated island of Deshima.

The Daughter, Anak Kompenie

If Van Nijenroode had not shipped all his belongings to Batavia, complete with a detailed inventory, the authorities would never have been able to lay hold of his property. The severity of the measures now taken was surely meant as a warning to all Company employees. The High Government was furious at the fact that the irksome Van Nijenroode had done so well for himself, especially during the trade embargo. The losers, of course, were Van Nijenroode's young daughters, Hester and Cornelia, who were left empty-handed.

The last wish of the deceased was that his daughters be given a Christian upbringing. The deputy chief in Hirado, Pieter van Santen, therefore wrote to the Governor-General and Council of the Indies (which together formed the High Government of Batavia) to say that he had set aside for this very purpose the 1,000 taels which the girls had inherited. Van Santen's wife was also of Japanese descent. She was the daughter of Melchior van Santvoort, a crew member of the *Liefde*—the first Dutch ship to arrive in Japan in 1600—who was still living with his family in Nagasaki. Other junior merchants and assistants in Hirado, such as Carel Hartsinck and François Caron, also lived with Japanese women. The courtyard of the Dutch trade factory was teeming with black-haired children.

Governor-General Hendrick Brouwer had nothing good to say about Pieter van Santen's behavior: the amount he had put aside for Hester and Cornelia's education was "truly impertinent." He reckoned that the girls could be put out to board with a foster family for less than 20 taels each. Considering that 1,000 taels, well-invested, could be counted on to yield eighteen percent interest, the Governor-General—who had very strong opinions about frugality—seemed to be insinuating that Van Santen was trying to bring up his own half-breeds with another man's money. He thought Van Santen "too young, too proud, and too arrogant, possessing traits completely at odds with the Japanese temperament" and recalled him to Batavia. Exit Van Santen and his family and with them the comfort and support, as well as the playmates, of the two Van Nijenroode girls.

Nicolaes Couckebacker of Delft was now appointed chief factor of the establishment in Hirado, and the instructions given him did not fail to include the standard sermon. The Governor-General warned Couckebacker not to have anything to do with the local ladies, because "the fathering of bastards degrades the pious nature of the Dutch." This advice went unheeded: Couckebacker himself would soon father two daughters with two different concubines.

The new chief factor obviously objected to carrying out his orders, which required him to take Van Nijenroode's children "away from their mothers and send them to Batavia." Cornelia was still too young, he wrote in his first letter to the High Government, and he gave an account of how the 1,000 taels had been spent. Van Santen had in fact deposited this amount in the factory's account, but only after deducting what had already been spent on the children's upkeep: a sum of 442 reales, which amounted to 1,386 guilders. This was an unbelievably large sum, considering that in those days an able-bodied seaman earned ten guilders a month. Couckebacker wrote that he regretted not being able to send the girls to Batavia because their mothers, Tokeshio and Surishia, were not yet ready to give up their children, unless, of course, the money due to them from the estate were paid in full. They felt they were entitled to it, especially after having given Van Nijenroode so much care and attention during his illness. From the evidence produced it also emerged that Van Santen, undoubtedly annoyed at the haggling of the High Government at Batavia, had personally guaranteed the payment of the entire amount.

While awaiting further instructions, Couckebacker reserved 30 taels for each girl, so that he could at least pay for their upkeep. After a three-year struggle, the council of Hirado decided on 24 September

1636 "to pay out the bequests, to take the girls from their mothers, and to send them to Batavia this year." However, because it was unclear whether special consent from the Japanese authorities was needed, more than a year went by before the children were put on board the Company ship *Galjas* at the end of November 1637. The Company acted as both judge and jury: first the girls had been denied their father's inheritance, now they were being taken away from their Japanese mothers to be raised in Batavia as Dutch girls. Both of them could rightfully be called *anak kompenie*, children of the Company.[3]

Hester and Cornelia were never to return to their native country. The shogun was determined to rid his land of Christendom once and for all. During the previous twenty years many Japanese Christians had been killed or forced to renounce their beliefs, and many others had fled to such overseas ports as Manila, Hoian (in Vietnam), and Batavia. All Japanese sojourning abroad were denied the right to return to their country. The first steps had now been taken to cut off the island empire from foreign influence.

Shortly afterwards the Portuguese traders in Nagasaki and their Japanese wives and children were ordered out of the country, and in 1639 the authorities announced that all Japanese women who had children with Dutch or English fathers would have to take their offspring and go to Batavia. Tokeshio and Surishia, the mothers of Hester and Cornelia, were spared this fate because their daughters had already left the country, and they themselves had meanwhile married Japanese men. It was further decreed that Japanese women would no longer be permitted to live with foreigners. This last regulation was not at all difficult to enforce, for after their move to Nagasaki in 1641 the Dutch found themselves in complete isolation on the little island of Deshima. Only a few courtesans were allowed to visit them in the evening "to make tea."

CHAPTER THREE

Portrait of a Marriage

Batavia is said to be a Paradise for women,
because they have the easiest time there.
—Elias Hesse,[1] 1690

It is not known who took care of Hester and Cornelia upon their arrival in Batavia, but in all likelihood the girls were committed to the Company's orphanage. Five years later, in 1643, Hester's name was recorded in the baptismal register of the Portuguese Church, the house of worship that opened its doors to ordinary folk because its services were conducted in Portuguese, the *lingua franca* of the town.[2] People from all walks of life felt at ease there: Christian Malays, baptized slaves, *Mardikas* (Malay for free Christians)—the latter were mostly Moluccans with elegant-sounding Portuguese names—mestizos, Dutch freeburghers, and even sailors of the fleet. The Protestant services at the Portuguese Church accommodated people of all denominations. No one looked askance at a Catholic, Lutheran, or Remonstrant background. Everyone was welcome.

Little is known of Hester's life, though the records show that she married twice.[3] The church register tells us that she appeared twice at the baptismal font of the Portuguese Church as godmother to infant children of her friends: in both cases the parents had come from

Hirado. There were relatively few Japanese or people of Japanese descent living in Batavia; altogether they numbered no more than three or four hundred. By far the majority of young people in this community married outside their own group. The lack of newcomers inevitably caused the Japanese colony to shrink, losing its specifically Japanese character in the process.

Cornelia van Nijenroode did not marry until 1652 at the age of twenty-three. The groom, Pieter Cnoll of Amsterdam, had arrived in Batavia five years earlier to work as a Company assistant on a salary of fifteen guilders a month. His thorough knowledge of bookkeeping had earned him, immediately after his arrival, a position in the Company cashier's office in Batavia Castle. That he performed well in this capacity emerges not only from the increase in his salary—as a junior merchant he was already earning forty-five guilders a month—but also from his rapid climb up the Company ladder. In 1657 this master bookkeeper was appointed cashier at the Castle on the condition that his own property serve as collateral, thereby holding him both personally and financially responsible for his work. Four years later Cnoll was promoted to second head merchant of Batavia Castle, and in the following year, upon promotion to first head merchant, he became responsible for the entire bookkeeping of the Company in Asia. A strict selection procedure ensured that only extremely dedicated and reliable men were chosen for this position. Though Pieter Cnoll was undoubtedly a first-class accountant, we should not assume that he was a typical pen-pusher. He was an extremely amiable fellow, whose star rose rapidly among the men of the civic guard: in 1658 he was appointed ensign, in 1661 he was promoted to lieutenant, and finally, in 1667, captain of the "Company's clerks at the Castle," in which capacity we see him portrayed with his militia sash in the portrait painted by Jacob Janszoon Coeman.

Cornelia gave birth to her first child, a daughter called Catharina, nine months after the marriage was solemnized. Over the next seventeen years she went on to bear nine more children, at intervals of one and a half to two years. Motherhood in the seventeenth century was generally a spasmodic cycle of pregnancies, deliveries, and burials, and Cornelia's experience of motherhood was no exception. When she wrote that letter to her mother Surishia in Hirado in 1671, only four of her children were still alive: Cornelis, Hester, Martha, and Elisabeth Catharina. Only Cornelis lived to adulthood, and Cornelia eventually outlived him as well.

Batavian Society

Pieter and Cornelia Cnoll moved in higher circles in the class-ridden colonial society of Batavia than Hester did, but they also had their share of Japanese connections. Again, a good yardstick is the baptismal register, this time that of the city's Dutch church, where the elite from the Castle and their wives attended services. When the Cnoll's son Cornelis was born, Susanna Schemon acted as godmother. She was one of the Japanese daughters of Nicolaes Couckebacker, the former chief factor of Hirado; her husband, Nicolaes Schemon, was the captain—or leader—of the Japanese community in Batavia. Naming the godfathers and godmothers of all ten Cnoll children would make for a long-drawn-out story, so let's take a look instead at a baptism that took place in 1658, because it gives a good indication of the social standing of the infant's parents. At the baptism of baby Hester, the ladies Femmetje Frisius–ten Broecke and Sara Hartsinck–de Solemne acted as witnesses. As a little girl Cornelia had sat on the knee of Sara's husband, Carel Hartsinck, who during his days as a merchant in Hirado had sired two boys with a Japanese concubine.[4] As in Cornelia's case, the boys' mixed descent did not prove a handicap. Pieter, the elder of the two, eventually earned a degree in theology from the University of Leiden and

Worshippers leaving the Dutch Church in Batavia after the Sunday service. (Johan Nieuhof, *Zee- en Lant-Reize*)

went on to become a counselor to the Duke of Brunswick. After a respectable career in the employ of the Dutch East India Company, Willem Carel occupied the post of governor of Coromandel, before retiring—a wealthy man—to a large country estate in Holland.

The relations between the Cnoll and Frisius families were no less revealing. As a special envoy of the Dutch East India Company, Andries Frisius had visited the Japanese court, and in 1658 he was secretary of the Council of the Indies and president of the Board of Matrimonial Matters and Small Claims. In the capacity of ensign of the

"Company employees outside the Castle," he was in frequent contact with Pieter Cnoll. On Frisius's recommendation, Cnoll was chosen, also in 1658, as captain of the Castle's clerks.

By this time the rank of militia officer had become more an honorary title than a position of real military significance. A candidate had to possess a certain bravura—in other words, he had to be a man's man—and have enough money to treat his men to an opulent banquet once a year when the city celebrated its founding. On that particular day, the men assembled at the home of the captain, where they were served a copious breakfast, after which the militiamen lined up, and the roll of the drums sounded the beginning of the parade. Marching along, the men stopped occasionally to present arms at the homes of the most prominent Company officials, who responded to this courtesy by offering them refreshment. After downing a stiff drink, the young heroes

The fish market (*pasar ikan*) with Batavia Castle in the background. (Tropenmuseum, Amsterdam)

fired a salute and marched off to the next address. Shortly after noon the company made its way to the parade ground between the city and the Castle, where the Governor-General and the members of the Council of the Indies took the salute and installed new officers, whom they then invited to empty a glass with them "in friendship, toasting the prosperity of our Fatherland, the East India Company, the city of Batavia, and anything else one could think of." Around sunset the men, already intoxicated, staggered back to the captain's house, "where, after firing several volleys in the air, they laid down their arms and spent the rest of the night in feasting and merriment." Pieter Cnoll must have carried out his duties with enthusiasm, doubtless letting his whole family take part in the festivities. He took the salute and inspected his men, standing with Cornelia and their children on the front steps of their house. And following him like a shadow was his faithful slave Untung with the banner of the militia slung over his shoulder.

Father Cnoll may have led an army of bookkeepers and militiamen, but Cornelia was no slouch either. As *mater familias*, she managed a household of more than forty slaves: slaves to guard the door, slaves to work in the kitchen, slaves to clean the house, slaves to do the shopping, *kebon* slaves to take care of the grounds, slaves to sew the clothes, slaves to mind the children—in short, slaves everywhere, both indoors and out. They were all jealous of one another's privileges and position within the household's hierarchy, and one can well imagine the iron hand necessary to command such an army. A stern mistress, Cornelia could deal with petty transgressions herself, but once in a while she was compelled—probably because the Batavian gossipmongers left her no choice—to report a serious breach of conduct to the Court of Justice. It was brought to her attention, for example, that one of her slaves, Jan of Bengal, "had committed a beastly sin," whereupon the unfortunate sinner, together with the dog that he had sodomized, were "thrown into the sea to drown."[5]

On weekdays Lady Cnoll went to tea parties, shopped at the cloth-

ing bazaar, or paid a visit to the Chinese porcelain vendor on the corner of Tea Street, always followed by two or three of her slaves: one
holding Pieter Cnoll's *payong* (parasol) above her head, one carrying
her betel box, and one bearing a basket or perhaps a *furoshiki*, a cloth in
which to wrap a present or costly purchase.

On Sundays the moment arrived when Cornelia could really play
the part of princess. Walking in the shadow of the large *payong*—the
privilege of the Batavian elite—and preceded by slaves carrying her
prie-dieu chair, betel box, and silver-clasped Bible, Cornelia appeared
on the arm of her husband Pieter at the entrance to the Dutch church.
At this point their paths parted: Cnoll took his place among the other

A well-to-do Batavian couple going for a ride *en carosse*. (Detail of a print reproduced in
Johan Nieuhof, *Zee- en Lant-Reize*)

merchants from the Castle, while his wife—dressed in sober black but laden with costly jewels—walked to her chair, which had been placed with those of the other ladies. Once installed, she gave a tap with her fan as a signal to her slaves to crouch down beneath the pulpit. She was then free to bask in her glory.

Another symbol of the status she had attained was the splendid coach that Cnoll had ordered from the carpenters of the craftsmen's quarter, coaches being the preeminent mark of conspicuous consumption in Batavia. In the early 1630s Governor-General Hendrick Brouwer had tried to suppress his countrymen's excessive show of wealth by prohibiting the use of coaches in the city. However, his successor, Anthonie van Diemen, took a more lenient approach, undoubtedly at the insistence of his luxury-loving wife Maria and her friends. In a letter to the Heren XVII, Van Diemen explained that he wanted to make a conciliatory gesture to the wives of the Castle's merchants, deprived as they were of the presence of their parents and other relatives, and often bereft of the attention of their husbands, who were constantly occupied with Company affairs. The coaches, which had been parked forlornly in a warehouse for several years, were now brought out of storage. He issued orders to "harness up the horses and get the coaches rolling, in the service of the ladies," so that "our beloved companions can enjoy some recreation and diversion in this melancholy climate," avoiding, moreover, "the unbearably hot sunshine when going to town to attend church on Sundays."[6]

In 1659, when peace was concluded with Bantam—the neighbor with which the Company had constantly been at odds since the founding of the city—the Batavian countryside was finally considered safe enough to build country mansions and pleasure gardens with summer houses. A burgher of high standing would naturally acquire a horse and carriage, but no one's carriage could compete with the splendid coach-and-four owned by Pieter and Cornelia. Appropriately enough, it had a golden turnip (knol, then spelled cnol, means turnip in Dutch) painted on its doors. On the old road to Jakarta, not far from the coast, Pieter Cnoll bought some land that he wanted to bring under cultivation, following the example of his neighbor, Pieter van Hoorn. Perhaps inspired by the reclamation of the Purmer polder back home in Holland, Van Hoorn, a scion of the Amsterdam patriciate, had committed to paper his ideas concerning the development of lands around the colonial city, strongly criticizing the "simple commercial pursuits" of the Company, which was not yet prepared to recognize the importance of tropical agriculture.[7] Pieter Cnoll was of a different opinion, but because he was far too occupied with Company business to take on the joys of country life, he decided, out of sheer necessity, to lease the whole piece of land—with the exception of a wooden house with greenhouses and a garden where he grew rosemary and other herbs and flowers—for twelve reales a month.[8] Here, at this idyllic retreat, Cnoll had himself, his family, and his home-grown flowers immortalized by the painter Jacob Janszoon Coeman.

Nostalgic Letters

After expelling all Dutchmen and their families, the Japanese took additional measures to prevent all correspondence between the exiles (including of course the Japanese expatriates living in Batavia) and their relatives living in Japan. Only in 1656 did the Japanese authorities relax this last measure and allow some exchange of family news, the so-called *on-shin*. Murakami Buzaeimon, for example, the "Japanese captain" of Batavia, was now able for the first time to send letters to the governor (*bugyo*) of Nagasaki, Kainosho Kizaemon—via the chief factor on the island of Deshima—with news of how the Japanese in Batavia were faring.[9]

The two letters from Cornelia to her mother Surishia were part of this exchange. They were discovered around a hundred years ago

The Tokugawa regime at first prohibited any contact between the Japanese living overseas and their relatives at home. This prohibition was cunningly disobeyed, as witnessed
by this so-called *Jakatara-bun* (Jakarta text), a letter smuggled into Japan. A certain
Koshioro in Batavia cleverly wrote it on pieces of cotton sewn together. (Kanko
shiryokan, Hirado)

among the personal belongings of a well-to-do family in Hirado.[10] Some
time after the death of Cornelis van Nijenroode, Surishia had married
a fellow townsman, Handa Goeimon, and had therefore been allowed
to stay in Japan. Cornelia's cautious letters perhaps tell present-day
readers less than they would like to hear, but by reading between the
lines one may glean something of the ups and downs of Cornelia's life.
A close translation of her first letter reads as follows:

Every year I receive the favors of both governors [*ryomandokoro*] of Nagasaki. Your letter from the twenty-first of the ninth month (of 1662) with the family news and presents was received in good order. I was very happy to hear that you are both in good health. I am sending with this epistle the following presents:

One piece of Chinese [illegible] for grandmother.

First-class refined Bornean camphor, weighing two catties [ca. three pounds].

Three pieces of striped Chinese cotton.

One pepper-and-salt-colored batik [chintz].

(The last three items are for Handa Goeimon.)

One gingham for Hester's mother.

Pepper-and-salt-colored chintz for my wet nurse.

Hamada Sukeeimon and his wife are very grateful for the many letters and goods they have received [from Nagasaki]. They are all in good health. I, Cornelia, can therefore live without worries. My husband Cnoll is a good man, and I get along with him better all the time. It is only a trifle, but I am also sending a roll of chintz to Yoshitsugi Kuzaeimon.[11] Would you please make sure he gets it? Forgive me, but would you send me six lacquer incense boxes and a comb of palm wood? Your devoted daughter, the twenty-first of the fifth month of the year 1663.

Cornelia Cnoll.

One of the two *on-shin* (exchange of family news) sent by Cornelia to her mother in Hirado. (Kanko shiryokan, Hirado)

From the correspondence it appears that there was some sort of regular exchange of family news, accompanied by a few presents. In any case, we are not told much about the Cnoll's family life.

The second letter was written eight years later to her stepfather Handa Goeimon. It is possible that other letters had been sent in the intervening period, though none has been preserved.

> Every year I receive many [favors] from the *bugyo* of Nagasaki. Your letter from the eleventh day of the ninth month of 1668, the list of gifts you requested, and the presents you enclosed arrived on the twenty-seventh of the tenth month. I've passed them on to everyone. They are all very happy and say they are embarrassed to receive so many gifts. Here in Batavia all is well. In the fourth month of last year [1670] I was delivered of a daughter. I now have four children, all of them healthy. You needn't worry. I am sending the following presents:
>
> > One roll of Salempore cotton, top quality.
> > One roll of *kanekijn* [cotton cloth from India], top quality.
> > One roll of narrow *kanekijn*.
> > Twenty-five rolls of Salempore cotton.
> > Twenty rolls of percale [cotton cloth from India].
> > Two rolls of chintz.
>
> The above-mentioned things are meant for the two of you. The roll of white cotton in one piece is for Hester's mother. The piece of percale is for my wet nurse.
>
> During the past two years, 1669 and 1670, nothing has been sent from here [Batavia] to Japan, so I assume you will be justifiably concerned. Fortunately, there is nothing wrong. I enjoy good health, you needn't worry about me. I have given birth to ten children, six of whom have died. Four are still living: the eldest, my son, is fourteen, his sisters are twelve and six years of age, and the youngest is only eight months old. All four are in good health. The eldest two in particular send their greetings to grandmother and grandfather. It always makes me happy to hear that you are still in good health. From your letters I have become acquainted with your living condi-

tions. Feeling as though I've seen you both, I wipe away my tears. Murakami Buzaeimon asks me to tell you that every year he has gratefully received your letters. Here in Batavia, *dai-feitor* (head merchant) Cnoll, his wife, and children are all in good health. But you are understandably worried because we haven't written for two years. His position as head merchant leaves him no free time whatsoever. On the one hand...[missing sentence]; on the other hand, the sale of [Company] goods are seen to by the *dai-feitor* alone. It is only a trifle, but I am sending you a roll of white silk woven with patterns.

Hamada Sukeeimon's widow says that, according to her records, she has received news every year. This makes her very happy. The whole of the Cnoll family, parents and children alike, are in good health. You will hear [further] details from Murakami Buzaeimondonne, so I will not write in detail here. Though it is but a trifle, I am sending a roll of white percale as evidence of my good health. [I hear that] grandmother died of an illness on the twenty-sixth day of the eighth month of 1668. I trust that she passed away peacefully like a good soul. Wishing you good health over and over again, I remain, on the twenty-first of the fourth month, your Cornelia Cnoll.

P. S. I forgot to write what I wanted to say first! To grandfather and grandmother I am sending another two rolls of Dutch worsted. They are from big brother and his sister [Cornelis and Hester], sent by both of them as a token of their affection. As regards the two rolls of white crêpe cotton I am sending along, would you please dye them deep red?

Cornelia's biggest worry, as emerges from these letters, was the health of her relatives, though the presents—the cotton fabrics from India— were also important to her. The obvious question is why she was sending bolts of cotton cloth to Japan. Part of the answer may lie in the strict edict issued in 1670 by Governor-General Maetsuycker.[12] According to this edict, in 1668 the rulers of the kingdom of Japan had given the chief factor of Deshima a list of articles that private individuals were forbidden to import into Japan. For the sake of "the welfare of the Company in general and that of our Company employees in particular" Maetsuycker felt compelled to allow "no one, no matter who, be they senior merchants, captains, junior merchants, mates, or any other persons, both officers and ordinary seamen" to export forbidden goods to Japan. This decree was followed by a detailed list of what the Japanese authorities considered to be forbidden exotica: worsted (woolen cloth from Holland), all kinds of Chinese silk, exotic animals, dogs, monkeys, birds, wood used for medicinal purposes, "Spanish flies, rat poison, and other toxins," glass, musical instruments, toys, Chinese tools, medical instruments, Dutch money, weapons, and especially any objects connected with the Christian faith, including, of course, the Bible. There was no ban on cats, however, because they were necessary to catch rats on board ship.

There was a hidden agenda in the prohibitory edicts of Japan's military regime, the *bakufu*. On the one hand, by restricting the import of exotic goods, the authorities, could reserve these same goods for the exclusive use of the elite. On the other hand, the import restrictions served to stimulate certain sectors of the domestic economy, thereby reducing dependence on foreign trade. To be sure, the decision to "close off" the country in 1640 had been made on both political and economic grounds: the *bakufu* was trying to create an autarky: a completely self-sufficient society in its own cultural sphere. As a result of these measures, porcelain and silk, which had previously been imported from China, were soon produced in such large quantities in Japan that before the end of the century it could provide enough of these products to meet its own needs. The sending of cotton cloth was not forbidden because cottonseed had been reintroduced into Japan by the Portuguese and Spanish a hundred years earlier, and thus cotton cloth was no longer considered a foreign product. In short, if Cornelia wanted to send presents to her relatives in Japan, she had little choice. At the same time, the ban on "paintings or any prints with Chinese characters, wherever they were made" explains why Cornelia chose such a singular method of sending a portrait of herself to her mother. Because the import of prints and paintings was forbidden, she sent a miniature wooden screen with the shape of a woman artfully cut out of it.

Cornelia's description of her husband and his business dealings also demands our attention, although a missing sentence prevents us from knowing exactly what she meant to say. (It just happens to be the sentence in which she tells of her husband's buying and selling activities.) One thing, however, is certain: Cornelia was telling the truth when she wrote that her husband, the first head merchant of Batavia Castle, was occupied day in and day out with Company business; various instructions in the Company's book of ordinances aimed at lightening his work load make this perfectly clear.[13] The Director-General (a subordinate of the Governor-General) was officially responsible for the bookkeeping at Company headquarters in Batavia, but because he was charged with extensive administrative duties, he delegated responsibility for the entire administration of Batavia Castle to the first head merchant. This official was required to share his duties with the second head merchant, which he did by assuming responsibility for the sale of goods and leaving it up to his colleague to buy the merchandise. Each of them was required to check the other's bookkeeping. But it was the first head merchant who bore the lion's share of the responsibility: he had the keys "to provide access by day or night, as the situation demands, to the Castle and the warehouses."[14]

Cornelia's husband may have been busy, yet he still found time, like an honest and upright family man, to preside over the Board of Matrimonial Matters and Small Claims.[15] Pieter Cnoll, it seems, was heading straight for a seat on the Council of the Indies, but before he could reach what would have been the pinnacle of his career, his health failed him.

The Will

At eight o'clock on the morning of 15 February 1672, after suffering all
night from a raging fever and excruciating pain, head merchant Pieter
Cnoll summoned to his bedside the notary Anthonie Huysman. The
patient, weakening fast, told the notary that he faced both "the certainty of death and the uncertain circumstances thereof."[16] Because he
did not know how long he would have his wits about him, Pieter Cnoll
asked the notary to draw up his will in the presence of his wife and the
merchants Pieter Pauw and Constantijn Nobel, two friends who were
keeping watch at his bedside. The will shows that the couple wanted to
be certain that the entire estate would go to the surviving spouse, without interference from outsiders. Cornelia, the disinherited orphan, was
now in her forties and an old hand at colonial life. She had no intention of being left behind empty-handed a second time: every detail had
to be correctly settled and duly recorded.

The notary wrote down that "all property, be it movable or non-
movable, claims, credits, debts outstanding, salaries or other monies,
nothing excluded, wherever they may be and from whomever they may
have been acquired" were to be allotted to the surviving spouse. She,
in turn, was required to assume responsibility for the care of the children, providing them with "food, drink, and clothing until they come
of age or marry" and also teaching them "to read, write, and learn a
decent occupation, enabling them to earn their own living." Marrying
or coming of age would give a child the right to the considerable sum
of 40,000 rixdollars, more than a million dollars in today's money.

The notary was then briefed on the Cnoll family's substantial fortune: there was more than enough to pay these legacies in cash. After
the notary had ascertained that this was indeed the case, he added a
clause to the will which stipulated that neither the regents of the
Orphans' Chamber nor anyone else would be allowed to interfere with
the execution of the will. Though he demanded that everything be set

down in writing, Pieter Cnoll expressly forbade any lists or descriptions of the inventory of his estate to be handed over to a third party.[17] His wife remembered all too well what had happened when the inventory of her father's estate had fallen into the hands of the authorities. Cornelia was designated in Cnoll's will as "the only and absolute guardian…and all this notwithstanding any statutes, ordinances issued by the Orphans' Chamber, or written laws to the contrary."[18] Cnoll alone was legally responsible for his offspring, and he now seized the opportunity to delegate this authority to his wife.[19] Cornelia was of course free to call in the help of one or more guardians. If one of the children were to die before receiving his or her legal share of the inheritance, this share would go to the surviving siblings. If all the children were to die prematurely, the entire inheritance would go to the surviving spouse, in this case Cornelia.

These were the most important points recorded by the notary on that early morning in February. Huysman asked Cnoll, his wife, and the witnesses to sign the document, whereupon he pocketed his fee of two rixdollars. To reimburse him for the expense of traveling to and from Cnoll's house, he was given an additional twenty stuivers.

The will had been drawn up just in the nick of time, for that afternoon the patient was again gripped by a raging fever, and two days later head merchant Pieter Cnoll breathed his last. On 20 February the Governor-General called a special meeting of the Council of the Indies to appoint a successor to the first head merchant.[20] They chose Cnoll's deputy, Gerrit Vrieslandt.

Now the moment had come to execute the will, the contents of which seemed on the surface to be perfectly straightforward. However, because there was no inventory, it was not clear, to start with, what should happen to the forty household slaves. Batavian slaveholders usually had a special clause inserted in their wills stipulating that their favorites—the slaves who had been closest to their master—be set free and that the others be given a small sum of money. Cnoll's failure to observe this custom would be bitterly regretted by Batavian society. His favorite servant and *payong*-bearer, Untung—the slave in the family portrait, standing in his master's shadow and depicted in the act of stealing an orange from a basket of fruit—was handed over years later to Cnoll's son Cornelis when the latter came of age. Untung appears to have been so ill-treated by his new master that he ran away. Some sources maintain that he was initially recruited as a commander of Balinese troops to police the Batavian countryside, but that he soon joined a band of runaway slaves who chose him as their leader. Emerging as a notorious robber chief under a new name—Surapati—he would cause the Dutch East India Company a great deal of trouble in the 1680s by joining the cause of the Javanese rebels.[21]

CHAPTER FOUR

Setting the Scene

I n 1673 the Heren XVII—the seventeen-member governing board of the Dutch East India Company—assembled in Middelburg for their autumn meeting. These meetings were usually held in Holland's capital, Amsterdam, though once every six years they were moved to the capital of Zeeland because the inhabitants of that proud island province

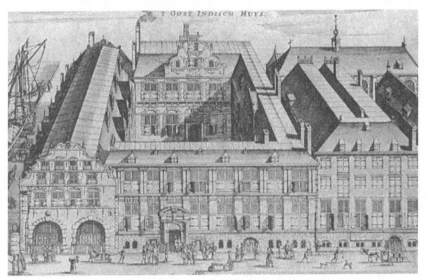

The East India house of the Amsterdam Chamber of the Dutch East India Company, situated at the corner of the Hoogstraat and the Kloveniersburgwal in Amsterdam. (*Zuid-Afrika's Geschiedenis in Beeld-Platen-Atlas*, Amsterdam 1913)

feared that the leadership of the Company was in danger of being dominated by their northern neighbors.[1] Important matters were discussed during this two-month meeting, for the young Dutch Republic was beset by difficulties.

A year earlier, in April 1672, England and France had declared war on the Republic. Luckily the country's navy had been ready to sail: on 25 May, near Sole Bay off the Suffolk coast, Admiral Michiel de Ruyter, aided by the flag officers who had accompanied him on his raid on the naval base at Chatham during the Second Anglo-Dutch War, dealt the first blow to the enemy. Although this temporarily reduced the likelihood of an allied landing on the Dutch coast, French and German troops nevertheless managed within months to occupy the country as far as the province of Utrecht.

The state in which the Dutch Republic now found itself has been aptly described in Dutch as *redeloos*, *radeloos*, and *reddeloos*. (The rabble was "unreasonable," the regents "desperate," and the Republic "beyond saving.") People began to clamor for the resignation of the leadership and the reinstallment of the Prince of Orange as supreme commander. On 2 July the States of Zeeland appointed Willem III, Prince of Orange, stadholder; two days later the States of Holland followed suit, and on 8 July the States General appointed him to the Captain- and Admiral-Generalship. Johan de Witt resigned as Grand Pensionary of Holland on 4 August, and less than three weeks later a frenzied mob in The Hague caught and brutally murdered De Witt and his brother Cornelis outside the Gevangenpoort, the prison where they had been detained on trumped-up charges of treason.

But nothing is so capricious as the business of war. The French campaign lost momentum and Louis XIV's troops were forced to mark time near the *waterlinie*—a large system of fortifications designed to flood half the province of Utrecht for defensive purposes—behind which the Prince of Orange had withdrawn with his troops. Even in December 1672, when an early spell of frost produced ice thick enough to support an entire army, the French troops still balked at crossing. This was enough to turn the tide of war during the winter months. In the spring of 1673 Willem III took the initiative. At first his sorties were nothing more than skirmishes, but as autumn approached, the military buildup was such that the Prince dared to attack the enemy in their own lines of communication. At sea things looked even better: Michiel de Ruyter had twice managed to defeat the combined naval forces of France and England; the siege was thus broken and access to the sea remained open.

The Heren XVII, meeting in Zeeland, could now take stock of the damages suffered by the Company in the preceding years. At first several ships returning from the Indies had sailed into the Channel only to be trapped by the English. There, thrashing about like fat ducks, they were captured straightaway by the enemy. Because the Company had to borrow money on the Amsterdam bourse to equip each outbound fleet and was therefore dependent on the profits of the return fleet to pay off its outstanding debts, this third Anglo-Dutch War had caused the Company considerable losses. Now that the sea routes had been reopened, the Heren XVII could get back to work. It was high time to send out a new Indies-bound fleet and draw up a list of goods to be ordered from the East. When they had dealt with these important issues and had agreed on the contents of the return cargo, the Heren XVII finally had time in the last two days of their autumn meeting to discuss less pressing matters, such as the appointment of the higher-placed administrative officials, the so-called qualified personnel of the Dutch East India Company.

All those proposed were appointed, with one notable exception: the middle-aged lawyer Johan Bitter, who on recommendation of the Amsterdam Chamber had applied for a seat on the Court of Justice at Batavia. His patron, Gillis Valckenier, a prominent member of the Amsterdam faction whose support of the Prince of Orange had earned him a renewed seat on the town council, had opted to stay in

Amsterdam and therefore missed the Middelburg meeting. And so, when it came time to vote, he was unable to support the candidature of his protégé.

The otherwise influential Valckenier was not especially popular with his fellow directors, and these gentlemen now saw an opportunity to thwart his designs. One member of the board did so by questioning the candidate's suitability, saying that a year or two earlier he had heard some things about Bitter that caused him to doubt whether he was actually the right man for the job. Moreover, the most important Amsterdam director present at Middelburg, Dirck Tulp, was on such bad terms with his fellow townsman Valckenier that he was in no mood to lend Bitter a helping hand. Because the meeting could not come to a unanimous decision—it was thought that Valckenier had not made the candidature attractive enough for the other directors—Bitter was advised to return to the capital and apply again in person to the Amsterdam Chamber. It was further decided that the Chamber could offer Bitter a position only after the rumors surrounding him had been thoroughly investigated.[2] The implicit message was that the candidate was being given a chance to preserve his dignity by withdrawing his application. Were the gentlemen correct in doubting Bitter's suitability for this responsible post?

The Young Lawyer

Johan Bitter was born on 20 September 1638 in Arnhem, the son of Arnolt Bitter and Aaltje Scholten, the daughter of a local barber-surgeon, Caspar Scholten. Father Bitter, who was already seventy-four at the time of Johan's birth, had no fewer than nine children from a previous marriage. He must have been hale and hearty, because after the birth of Johan he fathered two more children and eventually lived to the age of ninety-five, a remarkable achievement in those days. He died too soon, however, to witness the marriage on 1 August 1660 of his son Johan, still a student, to Bartha Eygels in the university town of Harderwijk.[3] The death of Johan's father did little to change the newlyweds' financial circumstances. Father Arnolt's estate was divided among all his children, and there was not much left for Johan. At any rate, a year and a half later, at the age of twenty-three, Johan Bitter received his doctorate in law from his Harderwijk alma mater.[4] The time had come for him to earn his own living, so the fledgling lawyer packed his books and took his wife and newborn daughter to Amsterdam, where he intended to set up his legal practice.

In these cosmopolitan surroundings, where concentric circles of canals were expanding yearly, Bitter could broaden his views. Coming into contact with people from all walks of life, he was confronted with a wide variety of legal problems and soon became aware of the enormous gulf between legal theory and judicial practice. Although not untalented as a lawyer, he was not quite able to distinguish between important matters and personal affairs of lesser consequence. This character trait was destined to determine the course of his career: whenever Johan Bitter was criticized, even in a trifling matter, he took great offense and did everything in his power to retaliate. Such hot-headed behavior naturally annoyed many of his acquaintances and colleagues, and his career as a lawyer suffered as a result.

His marriage, in the meantime, was proving to be more of a success. While still in Harderwijk, Bartha Eygels and Johan Bitter had produced their first child, a girl whom they named after Bartha. During the next ten years eight more children were born, one practically every year. Five of them died of childhood diseases, a picture quite similar to that of the Cnoll family in Batavia. The specter of infant death haunted Europe as well as the tropics.

Bitter's impetuosity may well have played a role in the decision he then made, or perhaps it was prompted by his inability to support such a large family. At any rate, Bitter decided—as many impecunious young men from good families have done before and since—to apply for a position with the Honorable Company and try his luck in the East Indies.

The Court of Justice at Batavia can best be described as the Supreme Court of the Dutch East Indies' colonial settlement. This judiciary body had had a difficult birth. At first, justice in the Indies was administered directly by the High Government, composed of the Governor-General and the Council of the Indies, in much the same way as the captain and his council administered justice on board an East Indiaman. There was no division of political and legal authority until 1620, when Jan Pieterszoon Coen installed "a board of commissioners or legal specialists within the Castle to try all simple lawsuits, be they criminal or civil." This judicial board—called the Court of Justice—was open to all civil and criminal cases brought before the board by soldiers or employees of the Company.[5] The Bench of Aldermen had jurisdiction over the freeburghers and "foreigners" in the town, who included, ironically enough, the indigenous population. In a few instances the Court of Justice at Batavia Castle functioned as a Court of Appeal for sentences handed down by the Bench of Aldermen.

Although in theory the Court of Justice acted as an independent court of law from 1620 onward, in practice things were very different indeed. Not only did the authorities often meddle in the judicial process, but personal ties continued to exist between the executive and the judiciary. The president of the Court of Justice, for example, was required to be a member of the Council of the Indies. Historical studies of the administration of justice in Batavia are filled with constant references to adjustments and amendments made over the years to strengthen and secure the freedom of action of the Court of Justice.[6] This positive development toward a properly functioning court of law was also evident in the rising standard of its members. To be sure, the Council originally consisted of "the most capable, senior ministers, who have learned much from life, and harbor a love of justice aimed at punishing evildoers and protecting the righteous," but one of the first members of the Court with an academic background in law called these upright citizens a bunch of "idiots and ignoramuses" led by "scoundrels and thieves."[7] This was the raw material the young court had to work with. Fortunately, the number of university graduates on the Court of Justice gradually increased, and by 1656 the majority of its members had an academic background in law.

As we have seen, the Heren XVII had their doubts about the character of the applicant Johan Bitter. Valckenier was furious when he heard how his protégé had been treated in Middelburg. His pride had been wounded by this "vote of no confidence," and as soon as Dirck Tulp returned to the capital, Valckenier called a special meeting of the Amsterdam Chamber to discuss the issue.[8] After a few inconsequential matters had been dealt with, Valckenier asked each man present whether he had anything to say about Bitter that might stand in the way of his appointment. This time no one dared raise an objection, and the candidate was invited to come into the assembly hall and introduce himself. Bitter was well prepared: he submitted three statements refuting the accusations brought against him at the meeting in Middelburg.

The first letter he produced was a recommendation signed by the six most senior solicitors in the city, as well as two barristers. They let it be known that not only was he "well grounded in jurisprudence" but that they also considered him "modest, peaceable, and sincere" in both public and private life. In short, they could think of nothing that stood in the way of his appointment to the Court of Justice. The other letters dealt with the rumors in circulation. It appeared that several years previously Johan Bitter had quarreled with a physician, a certain Hendrick Houtappel, about a bill. This matter had eventually been settled through the mediation of two aldermen, who had determined that the argument was nothing but a misunderstanding arising from mistakes made on both sides. At any rate, the affair had finally blown over. The good doctor Houtappel had even been willing to testify, in the presence of a notary, that it had all been one big misunderstanding, adding that he found Bitter to be "an honest and trustworthy lawyer" and that he bore him no grudge whatsoever.

After going over each item, Valckenier decided it was time to wind up the matter. He asked all those present if they had anything else to say and could not refrain from adding "especially anything prompted by the considerations voiced by Mr. Tulp." No one had anything to say. Even Mr. Tulp let it pass, and so Bitter was appointed to a seat on the Court of Justice at a monthly salary of 100 guilders.[9] Now that his employment by the Company had been settled, thanks to the intervention of Gillis Valckenier, Bitter began preparations for the long and dangerous voyage to the Indies: dangerous, not only because so many ships were lost on the way, but also because it was a risky undertaking to travel with a pregnant wife and small children, who were particularly susceptible to the epidemics frequently occurring on board.

Life Begins at Forty

In mid-December 1674 Johan Bitter, his wife, and five children braved the winter weather and boarded a small yacht which conveyed them to the island of Texel, where the outbound fleet of eight ships lay at anchor, waiting for a favorable east wind to carry them safely past the Haaks shoals to the open sea. The lawyer and his family boarded the *Ceylon*, the largest East Indiaman of the fleet. Johan Bitter decided to keep a journal of the voyage, suitably titled *Breviarum ab inito mari oceano*. On the first page of his journal he wrote this opening line, part of which he borrowed from the Book of Revelation (1:8): "Our beginning came to pass in the name of the Lord, who is 'Alpha and Omega, the beginning and the ending.'" From the jottings on the first pages of this travelogue, it is obvious that Bitter had devoted some study to maritime matters, having drawn up a neat list of wind directions, useful tips

about weights and measures, and some information on such diverse subjects as coins, precious stones, and gunpowder.

The naval war between the Dutch Republic and England had just
come to an end, so there was no longer any danger of being captured by
an enemy ship. An easterly wind was all the East Indiamen needed to
ensure swift passage through the Straits of Dover. As protection from
the Dunkirk privateers, the ships were to be escorted by Rear Admiral
Engel de Ruyter, son of the famous naval hero. They were forced to wait
for a favorable wind, however, and it was not until 24 January 1675 that
the "very valuable fleet, after a slow start, finally managed with the help
of an easterly wind, around nine o'clock in the morning, with clear
skies and a favorable breeze, to clear the Texel straits and put out to
sea," upon which the ships were lined up in a convoy. Off Petten, however, the wind changed to westerly and shortly afterwards died down
altogether. It was decided to drop anchor, as otherwise the flood tide
might drive the ships dangerously close to the coast.

The landlubber Bitter was fast becoming acquainted with the perils
of travel by sea. That very evening—although the ship was riding at
anchor and well lit—a merchantman suddenly drifted out of nowhere
across the bow of the Ceylon. It was only because the captain had the
presence of mind to cut the hawser, allowing the Ceylon to float free,
that the damage was limited to a few scratches on the ship's hull.
Scarcely recovered from the shock, the crew cast the other anchor and
the ship was soon secured again. Clearly, they were not making any
headway. When the admiral gave the command at nine o'clock to set
sail again, the anchor was weighed, but the ship tacked about the wrong
way and threatened to drift onto the shoals, so the anchor was again
dropped "out of great fear of the Haaks." Fortunately the plumb-line
showed twelve and a half fathoms, so there was more than enough
water under the heavily laden ship. The next day the wind changed to
northerly, but now the hawser was pulled so taut, owing to the combined strength of the wind and the southward-moving tide, that they

could no longer turn the capstan. Not until the next morning did the crew succeed at long last in weighing anchor, by now considered "half lost." That evening everyone on board was relieved to see the other ships in the fleet sailing into view.

The whole of the Bitter family, with the exception of Arnolt and Mother Bartha, had lain seasick in their bunks these last few days, but now their appetites began to return. That evening, wrote Bitter, "I sat at table but we had to hold on to the plates in order to eat." On 28 January Calais was sighted to leeward, but the fleet had scarcely passed the white cliffs of Dover when the wind backed to southwesterly, forcing them to change course for Plymouth. During the week and a half that the fleet and three other Dutch convoys spent at Plymouth, all kinds of business matters were dealt with on shore by the Company's local representative, William Jennings. Several soldiers and sailors also took advantage of the delay and deserted. After the convoy had again set sail, it found itself the following day in such a terrible storm "that everything was falling over, we were even afraid the ship would capsize!" Three days later, when the storm had blown over and Cape Finisterre was sighted, Rear Admiral Engel de Ruyter came on board the *Ceylon* one last time to take his leave. The captains of all thirteen ships in the convoy were now invited on board to set the course for the Cape Verde Islands.

In the Bay of Biscay the ship once again ran into stormy weather. More than a week later, Bitter and his wife both became so ill that they took to their bunks for several days, "sick and weak, she in a box bed and I in the bunk." On 3 March Bartha "was very opportunely delivered, around six bells in the dog watch, of a dead child, a boy," wrote the father, apparently much relieved that his wife had survived seasickness, exhaustion, and childbirth.

But it was not to be, for after dipping his quill in the ink again, Bitter continued: "Then [my wife]—through the negligence of the barber-surgeon, who was unable to remove the afterbirth—sadly passed away around three bells in the afternoon watch." All this took place while Bitter himself was running a high fever, having been "in a burning heat" for more than a week. As was only to be expected, he began to despair of his own recovery and on 4 March, assisted by junior merchant Dirck Steenhoven, Bitter drew up his last will and testament, "for the sake of the welfare of my five dear children." During the days that followed he was racked with a burning fever, and during a hurricane on 8 March Bitter thought his hour had come. While the storm raged he called Steenhoven again to help him write farewell letters to the directors of the Company and to his best friends at home. For more than a week the patient lay delirious in his bunk, his illness not abating, when suddenly on 17 March there were signs that he might recover after all. "Through a miraculous alteration, all at once I began to sweat, and this has given me a good deal of relief. I have rested as I have not been able to do since 27 February," he noted in his journal. Three days later his appetite actually began to return, and when "land ho!" was shouted from the crow's nest in the early morning of 23 March, he came on deck to see the Cape Verde Island of Maio with his own eyes. Bitter had arranged with the captain that as soon as the ship lay at anchor his wife's body would be taken on land and buried, and this was duly carried out the following day around four in the morning.

The short stopover was a good opportunity to write more letters to send home with returning ships. Bitter undertook this task with so much energy that he soon had to retire to his bunk to recover from the effort. At the nearby island of São Tiago the fleet again dropped anchor with the intention of taking on "fresh water, root vegetables, and berries." This proved to be more difficult than expected. The Dutch were told that they would be given water only if they agreed to buy goats and cows and pay anchorage dues. Bitter again felt so wretched he thought he was doomed. He dragged himself back to his cabin and, at his wits' end, committed his innermost feelings to paper, begging the

Lord for forgiveness. On this occasion Bitter chose to express his thoughts in Latin:

> I have at least done one thing: I have recalled all the serious sins committed since my childhood, as well as all the other false steps I have taken, and confessed and tearfully lamented them from the very depths of my soul. Admitting that I am unworthy, I have thrown myself on God's mercy, begging for forgiveness from the bottom of my heart, in the name of Jesus Christ, His dearly beloved Son, my only Savior, whom I recognize through my faith to be my certain redeemer, asking that the granting of forgiveness be made known to me through the Holy Spirit.

Johan Bitter took a deep breath. He had managed to say it, and after this outpouring of emotion he was overwhelmed by a feeling of relief, finally at peace with himself and the world around him. He blew out the candle and fell fast asleep, waking up the following morning with the strength to write, "Last night I slept so well that it seems to have been a night of deliverance."

As fate would have it, now that Bitter was able to clamber out of his sickbed, his assistant Dirck Steenhoven fell ill. One afternoon two weeks later, while the ship drifted aimlessly in the doldrums, Steenhoven breathed his last. His eyes were closed by Bitter, who had kept watch beside him till the end.

But what had become of the children in the meantime? During the weeks their sick father had kept to his bunk, the eldest daughter Bartha —herself only fourteen—had taken care of her little brothers and sisters like a mother hen, and she would continue to do so throughout the voyage.

And what about the ship? Becalmed in the doldrums, the ship, its sails flapping, continued to ride the ocean swell. For ten days running it had progressed no more than 12 to 20 miles a day. It was enough to drive one mad. On 28 April the steward, Pieter Blom of Rotterdam—

who may have drunk too deeply from his own barrel—could stand it no longer and leapt overboard, "without anyone having given him the slightest cause to do so." Not long after this incident the *Ceylon* was picked up by the trade winds, and two months later, on 22 June, the ship reached Cape Town, where fresh provisions were laid in for the crew, most of whom were suffering from scurvy.

On 8 July the anchor was again weighed. Judging from the records, the cross-

The "atonement", or *apologia pro vita sua*, written by a critically ill Johan Bitter. (Journal kept on board the *Ceylon*, N.S.M., Amsterdam)

ing which followed, from Cape Town to Batavia, must have been a nightmare. No fewer than thirteen seamen, fourteen soldiers, and two passengers died en route.[10] On 6 September the volcano of Krakatoa was sighted in the Java Straits, and six days later, via Bantam, the fleet reached Batavia. Upon disembarking, the Bitter family was conveyed to temporary lodgings in Batavia Castle. The 38-year-old lawyer (in the tropics this was more or less retirement age) found himself at the beginning of a new career and a new life in the East. For the time being his eldest daughter, little fourteen-year-old Bartha, was his only help and consolation.

The Court of Justice at Batavia consisted at this time of nine members, including the president. Most of them held other posts within the Company hierarchy and this provided them with extra income from emoluments. With five young children to take care of, Bitter had every reason to worry about his financial situation. It was not long before the newcomer realized that his monthly salary was not nearly enough to provide for himself and his offspring. He must have been shocked to discover that the cost of living in the colonial city was twice as high as in Holland.[11] His future would have been bleak indeed if one of his colleagues had not pointed out a "middle-aged" widow with "her own house—large, magnificent, well-furnished, and amply supplied with silver—attended to by about forty slaves, male and female, and possessing moreover a coach and horses." It is not difficult to guess who fit this description.[12] At any rate, Johan Bitter decided to take his daughter Bartha into his confidence. He told the poor girl that he would soon release her from the burden of caring for her younger brothers and sisters, for he was planning to remarry.

Courtship

The way in which Johan Bitter courted Cornelia van Nijenroode was later described so graphically by Cornelia's lawyer that it would be a shame not to quote part of his text here:

> And then having seen how well the plaintiff was situated, and
> himself understanding that a well-filled purse would serve his needs
> exceedingly well and an opulent household aid him in his appoint-
> ed function, he fell in love with the plaintiff's fortune, and having
> become acquainted with her through the agency of good friends, he
> began to court her and managed to be so persuasive, with his pretty
> words and promises, that she, the plaintiff, resolved to marry him.[13]

What would possess a wealthy 46-year-old widow, who had already lost all her children except her eldest son, to marry a man eight years her junior? Was she in love with him, or did she have other reasons? Judging from the conditions she insisted on including in the marriage settlement, it must have been a marriage of convenience. Bitter's academic background and his high social standing as a member of the Court of Justice attracted Cornelia greatly: this man would restore her to her position in society. He might be short of money, but his high rank opened up a whole range of possibilities that were denied to a "woman alone." Moreover, a marriage with him would once again open the doors of the Castle. The most important factor, however, was undoubtedly Bitter's seat on the Court of Justice. This would provide Cornelia with the legal footing she urgently needed to continue her business dealings; people would think twice before trying to cheat a woman in her position.

Cornelia very likely entertained these thoughts, as evidenced by comparable behavior seen in other colonial societies during this period. In Latin America, for example, Creole women of good breeding were standing in line to marry judges. This raised their status and "afforded all kinds of opportunities to use their husbands' influence."[14] Similar developments were seen in Portuguese India: judges and senior officials often married extremely wealthy Eurasian women, even though this practice was regularly forbidden by royal decree.[15]

Cornelia was well aware of the risk she was taking in marrying Johan Bitter. Although she was probably unable to anticipate all the legal consequences, she must nevertheless have known that she was placing herself in a subordinate position. After all, Dutch law gave the husband complete control over his wife. Cornelia would therefore be under the guardianship of Johan Bitter, who would exert complete authority over both her person and her property. The husband's control of his wife's assets had two important aspects: first, only the husband was allowed to enter into contracts and take legal action; second, he was in charge of managing his wife's fortune. In practice this enabled the husband to dispose of his wife's possessions without her permission and to make use of them as he saw fit. It was therefore not a bad idea for a wealthy woman who was thinking of marrying to have a document drawn up beforehand, a prenuptial agreement known as a marriage settlement, which was intended to prevent possible mismanagement on the part of her future husband. It was no more than a defensive measure, applicable only in the worst of cases, and should not be seen as a legally binding document giving the woman the right to act on her own, as this was by definition impossible.

Cornelia, the middle-aged bride-to-be, left nothing to chance, enlisting the help of advisers to create a watertight contract:

> She declared . . . that she was and would remain the legal guardian, mistress, and administrator of all her assets and property, present and future, with none excepted, in order to dispose freely of the same, buy and sell, invest, mortgage, and dispose of them at her own discretion.[16]

Indeed, it was customary—and Hugo Grotius refers to this in his *Introduction to Dutch Jurisprudence*[17]—to allow a woman "who was in the habit of baking or brewing" to continue working after marriage, and likewise a married woman who "publicly conducted a trade or business" to continue doing so at her husband's discretion. Bitter, however, must have pointed out to Cornelia's advisers that she could not go on buying and selling goods and property without his explicit permission, and that such permission would be forthcoming only after the marriage had been solemnized.[18]

The conditions stipulated in the marriage settlement, which had to be signed prior to the marriage ceremony, severely limited the freedom of action of Cornelia's new husband. But this was made up for in other ways. The bride promised the groom the sum of 25,000 rixdollars should she die before he did. If he were the first to die, his children would receive 12,500 rixdollars. According to the contract, however, the groom himself would receive nothing in cash. The interest on the money reserved for Bitter, to which Cornelia added an extra amount, would be used to support the married couple and their household. For his part Bitter agreed to contribute 5,000 rixdollars and his monthly income, including all his extra earnings. If this was not enough to cover their daily expenses, Cornelia would make up the deficit out of her own purse.

Because Cornelia was still not certain whether she had the absolute right to manage her own assets as she saw fit, she demanded—rather pathetically, it seems—that her future husband swear "that his intentions in marrying her had nothing to do with her fortune, but stemmed only from pure and heartfelt love for her and from his concern to provide a good upbringing for the children from his first marriage."[19]

The matter was settled on 7 March 1676. In the presence of the notary Davidt Disponteyn the marriage settlement was signed without further ado. The only dissonant note was sounded by the groom, who had managed to scrape together only 3,750 rixdollars instead of the 5,000 agreed upon. Cornelia van Nijenroode and Johan Bitter were married three weeks later, on 26 March 1676, just six months after Bitter's arrival in Batavia.[20]

CHAPTER FIVE

Give and Take

When young wine, confined too closely,
Grieves and suffers, grieves and chafes,
Without breathing, suffocates,
See how it wells up most grossly,
See how rank the floor's become,
With vapors rising from the scum.
—Jacob Cats[1]

The honeymoon was not yet over when Cornelia revealed her plan to invest 3,000 rixdollars in a house being built for a Chinese doctor near the Nieuwe Poort. She wanted the contract drawn up in her own name, so that the interest would be payable to her personally and would not end up in the joint account she shared with her husband. The Bench of Aldermen who were required to declare the contract legally binding refused to allow this on formal grounds as long as Cornelia's husband had not given her permission to act as a "public tradeswoman."[2] Nothing seemed to stand in the way of such a declaration, but to everyone's surprise Bitter refused to cooperate with the plan. He said that his wife had not informed him of the transaction beforehand and added that, although she might not have realized it, there was nothing in the marriage settlement saying that he would not

be allowed to administer Cornelia's property. The only freedom left to
her, he remarked archly, was "to give such orders as she wished in her
last will and testament," in other words, to stipulate in her will who
would receive her property after her death. This was scant consolation
to Cornelia, who was feeling quite fit and not at all ready to trade the
temporal for the eternal. Her new husband was in fact letting her know
that from now on he had the freedom to do what he liked with her
property. Bitter had also set his sights on the splendid coach-and-four
in Cornelia's stables. He could already see himself riding through town
to work. This coach, however, now turned from a dream come true into
a bone of contention.

François Valentijn, the late-seventeenth-century author of *Oud en
Nieuw Oost-Indiën* (The Old and New East Indies), heard the following
anecdote upon his arrival in Batavia in the 1680s: Cornelia and Johan
had not been married long before they had a quarrel, arising from
Cornelia's discovery that Johan had commissioned a local artisan to
paint over the turnips that decorated both doors of her coach and to
replace them with his own coat of arms. Cornelia was appalled. The
lady of the house had no objection to her husband's going out for a ride,
but his desire to erase the memory of the late Pieter Cnoll from "their
coach" was going too far. "The turnip had indeed turned bitter" was
Valentijn's clever comment on the situation.[3]

The scales fell from Cornelia's eyes, and she began to realize that all
the toadying and flattery of the preceding months had had but one
goal: "her person had indeed been the object of [Bitter's] show of words
and promises, but her fortune and belongings had been the object of his
innermost desires." She complained to anyone who would listen that
Bitter's outward display of affection and conjugal visits had become less
frequent, only to cease altogether a short time later. Worse still, his lack
of interest in her, at first expressed as "displeasure and nastiness," had
later degenerated into "harsh and unbearable treatment."[4]

Bitter did not take Cornelia's reproaches quietly. He retaliated by telling everyone that his new wife did not know where to draw the line. According to him, she was the proverbial wicked stepmother, taking out her frustrations on his children, who had moved with him into her house. There may well have been some truth in this. Cornelia had lost all of her children except her son Cornelis, and this probably made it difficult for her to bear the presence of her new husband's young children. In particular, she was constantly falling out with Bartha, who always stood up for her younger brother and sisters. The situation became intolerable when little Johanna died, after which Johan Bitter felt compelled to find lodgings for his remaining offspring with another family.[5] This was an especially hard blow, since one of the reasons he had decided to remarry was his hope that Cornelia would act as a second mother to his children and give them a good upbringing.

Before long it became impossible to keep the newlyweds' quarrels private. Everyone was scandalized by the screaming and fighting that went on at their house, drowning out the crickets in the tropical evenings and keeping the whole neighborhood in thrall. Less than half a year after the wedding, the church council felt it necessary to investigate the matter. Two of Bitter's colleagues on the Court of Justice, Cornelis Speelman and Constantijn Ranst, were chosen as mediators. Their intervention did in fact lead to a new agreement and the affair seemed to quiet down for a while. The choice of these two gentlemen had been a deliberate one. Ranst, a distant relative of Gillis Valckenier (Bitter's patron), was married to Hester Hartsinck, who—like Cornelia —had a Japanese mother and had been born in Hirado. This meant that Ranst was just the sort of trusted adviser Cornelia was likely to listen to. Cornelis Speelman had long been a good friend of hers, having been Cnoll's predecessor at Batavia Castle and a frequent visitor to their home.

The two advisers quickly came to the conclusion that Cornelia had kept her husband on too short a financial leash. They persuaded her to "hush up and suppress further troubles" by giving Bitter a lump sum in cash and bonds worth 25,000 rixdollars, the amount that the marriage settlement stipulated would be his if she were to die before he did. Their advice must have been something along these lines: "Give the poor devil a substantial sum so that he doesn't have to come begging every time he needs money." So it was ordained, and even though the notary determined that, should Bitter die before his second wife, his children would have to repay half the money, Bitter went along with these measures. It was—at least for him—a step in the right direction.[6]

In this way Johan Bitter was given direct control of the princely sum that had been dangled in front of him like a carrot before the wedding. It was decided, however, that Cornelia would manage her remaining assets as she saw fit; in other words, she could invest her money and conduct business in her own name. Bitter's four children would leave Cornelia's house and go to board "with honorable people," and the not inconsiderable expenses incurred by these measures—100 rixdollars a month—would be paid out of their joint household account. Cornelia could live with this: she would rather spend money on their board than have those noisy children in the house. Just over six months after signing the marriage settlement the couple signed a new "cohabitation contract."[7] To ensure that neither party would try to back out of the agreement later, a proviso was added at the last minute, stating that "all this has been arranged and concluded in love and friendship to promote harmony and to avoid all foreseeable troubles."[8]

Within a week 13,000 rixdollars in sealed bags and another 12,000 rixdollars in bills of exchange redeemable by the Company were handed over to Johan Bitter, who declared himself satisfied with the transaction. Suddenly he was a rich man. Cornelia now thought that peace had been restored and trusted she would in future "be able to live in harmony" with her husband. For a while this even seemed to be the case. Bitter wrote exuberant letters to his friends in Holland and told them that, after losing his wife on the voyage to the Indies, in Batavia he had remarried and was living in comfortable circumstances, having acquired a very rich wife—a widow with a son—and he had money, property, and rank in good measure. His marriage was a blessing, and he was satisfied with his financial situation. (His friends had doubtless gleaned as much from his letters and those of others.) "[He] lived in a magnificent house, with money as plentiful as shells, horses as strong as iron, and a coach fit for a king."

When his boasting "and other extravagant expressions" later came to light, it was remarked that this sort of scribbling "was unseemly for a man of his years in such a position."[9] Indeed, it was rather tasteless for a man of rank.[10] When he was reproached on this score Bitter did not deny that he had written the letters, but commented with a shrug of his shoulders that "even the most distinguished gentlemen had at times written facetious missives." One thing Bitter probably had not mentioned in these letters was that his wife had given him a rapier and a cane with a gold handle as wedding presents—symbolic gifts that he would use for better or worse as time went on.

At any rate, now that peace had returned to the Bitter household Cornelia took up her business activities with renewed vigor. She issued a bond worth 500 rixdollars payable to a certain Captain Verbeek and provided the previously mentioned Chinese doctor with a mortgage of 3,000 rixdollars to enable him to build his house at last.[11]

Domestic Life

The peace treaty unfortunately turned out to be no more than a temporary cease-fire. Once again the marital tempers flared. At a distance of three hundred years it is not easy to determine what exactly took place at that house on Tiger Canal. It is known, however, that Bitter snubbed Cornelia's sister Hester in all manner of ways. Whenever the mood seized him, he scolded her and also took delight in imitating her voice. With his newly acquired cane he chased his stepson Cornelis out of the house, screaming that he would drive his rapier through him if he did not hand over his horse immediately. He also suffered bouts of destructiveness, during which he threw bottles and candlesticks around the house. Once he even threatened to hack the coach to pieces.

This information is based on judicial sources containing the words of both plaintiff and defendant.[12] While it is tempting to reproduce in their entirety these juicy descriptions from the court records, there is no point in quoting Bitter's pronouncements literally if one cannot see them in a broader context. On closer inspection Bitter's tirades prove not to have been a random series of insults. If we consider the social environment—Batavia's multiracial colonial society with its hierarchical structure—then the stream of abuse Bitter poured on Cornelia offers a rather revealing picture of the norms and values obtaining at that time in Batavia. Cornelia's lawyer, who many years later would sum up all of Bitter's insulting remarks for the Court of Holland, naturally did so in order to underscore what a despicable person he was. But first let us examine Bitter's tactics and see just why his behavior was so insulting.

Cornelia was subjected daily to very bad treatment indeed. Bitter called her names like "whore-madam, beast, she-devil, and everything ugly," only to regain his self-control and suddenly say, "Come on, old girl, let's make peace." If Cornelia did not greet this proposal with a satisfactory reply, he immediately resumed his ranting and raving, calling her a "beast, whore-madam, and harlot." Sometimes he even threatened her with the sjambok, a heavy whip used to flog slaves. Stamping his feet with rage, he yelled in the presence of all the slave-girls in the house, "You Godforsaken beast, you're nothing but a whore!" He confided to the cook that her mistress was "nothing but a beast, I'm sorry I ever married her." He called the slaves together and ordered them not to listen to their mistress, telling them she hadn't the heart to beat them, and if she did, they should come and find him in the town hall or wherever he was and he would protect them.[13]

Bitter's hateful behavior followed a clear course as he systematically humiliated his wife in the presence of her own servants. Inciting household slaves to rebel against their master or mistress was considered the greatest possible humiliation in colonial society, because no slave would take a mistress seriously once she had been ridiculed by her peers. Moreover, Bitter even harangued Cornelia's lady friends. One day when a number of them were visiting, Bitter suddenly came into the room carrying a mirror. He held it in front of his wife's face and scoffed at her, saying, "Look at this gem," adding that he would rather have lost his arm than be married to her.

Bitter also called his wife a "black devil-face," undoubtedly referring to her Japanese features. All these tactics—threatening his wife with a whip, belittling her in the presence of the slaves, and encouraging them to ignore her orders—were of course devastating for a woman who depended on more than forty slaves to run her household.

On 29 September—only two weeks after signing their new contract—Cornelia fled from the hell on earth that had once been her home. She spent the night at the home of her son Cornelis, who had already been driven out of the house.[14] When she returned home the following day, her husband hurt her so badly, she claimed, that he dislocated her shoulder. As proof of this she showed Reverend Pays a statement written by her doctor. Two "independent" doctors, summoned in great haste by Bitter, made a completely different diagnosis, however, maintaining that they could not find one bruise on her body. Which party was being truthful is neither here nor there: the scandal was now out in the open.

At last the church council took action. It was the duty of the Court of Justice to inflict heavy punishments when crimes were committed, but it was the pastoral duty of the church to settle marital disputes like this one. During a meeting of the church council preceding a celebration of the Lord's Supper, Reverend Pays reported that he had paid Johan Bitter a visit after hearing his wife's complaints. His attempts to

patch things up between them had been unsuccessful: Bitter had coolly declined all offers of help.

Pays had not yet come to the end of his story when the door flew
open and Bitter himself burst into the room. Seething with anger, he
protested bitterly against the reverend's meddling in his marital quarrel
and the disciplinary measures the church council was planning to take.
He could not believe the assembled gentlemen were serious in their
resolution to suspend his presence at the Lord's Supper, without asking
anyone else how matters stood and without hearing what he had to say
on the subject.[15] Indeed, this was not how things were done in a real
court of law. In a case of ecclesiastical censure, however, the accused
was not permitted to ask for counsel, nor was he shown any evidence
or even told the names of his accusers. He had no choice but to accept
the church council as a judicial body, even in his dispute with the reverend. Bitter found the ways of the Lord mysterious indeed!

He challenged all those present to speak out against him. No one, of
course, was willing to do so. When the irate husband had finally been
removed from the room, the elders deliberated upon the proper
response to his presumptuous behavior. They decided to ban both
Bitter and his wife from the Lord's Supper. Neither would they tolerate
further provocations. Bitter was called into the room and notified of
their decision. Not fazed in the slightest, he challenged them all to
appear "before the Heavenly Tribunal" and then stormed out of the
room.[16]

Now that he had declared war on the church council, Bitter pulled
out all the stops, using his knowledge of law to wage war in public. In
the presence of others he directed "very rude and foul language" toward
his wife and made "all sorts of grimaces: pulling faces, sticking out his
tongue, and crossing his eyes." He also tried to dig up some dirt from
Cornelia's past. In the archives of the secretary of the Council of the
Indies he found a lot he could use. Waving the documents he had discovered, he told anyone who would listen that his wife's father "had

sold his Godforsaken soul to the devil" and that his possessions had been confiscated.

Bitter, who obviously no longer felt safe at home, barricaded his room and armed himself with "a heavy pestle, a rice-pounder, and a large wooden maul." In early October, when Cornelia returned home, he hired a bodyguard, who even accompanied him to the dinner table, probably in order to test his food for poison. With renewed energy he repeatedly tried to damage his wife's reputation and deprive her of her friends. One evening he stormed into Cornelia's bedroom, where she was talking to a lady friend. He was wearing only "an undershirt and drawers, [he was] barefoot, without shoes or slippers, [and he had] a rapier in his hand." He had probably assumed that his wife was entertaining a male visitor.[17]

Finally, the Bitter residence was closed to all visitors. One afternoon in November Cornelia, who had invited some ladies to tea, found her husband at the front door, refusing to let her guests enter. When she saw the ladies hesitating, she begged them to stay, saying, "Ladies, please come in, I asked you to my house for a cup of tea." The ladies quickly retreated, however, when her husband burst out, "*Your* house, it's *my* house, I've sold it and I'll see that it gets handed over to its new owner."

Having already been deeply humiliated in the presence of her slaves, Cornelia was now the victim of Bitter's brutish behavior in the presence of her friends. Little by little the inventive Bitter refined his tactics. He promised Cornelia a divorce if she would pay him 50,000 rixdollars in cash. He would then "go back to Holland, where he could live like a king on that trifling sum."[18] During the last days of November the couple was involved in such a caustic quarrel that once again Cornelia was forced to flee.

Taking flight from her own home did not mean that Cornelia had admitted defeat. She called on friends to help her and prepared for a frontal assault on her husband. She had discovered, in fact, that Bitter had spent part of his newly acquired riches on diamonds and had sent them to Holland on board the East Indiaman *Europa*, which had sailed from Batavia on 11 November. Cornelia came to hear—probably from former subordinates of her late husband—that Bitter had sent another 3,000 rixdollars to Holland by means of a bill of exchange payable to his friend Jacob Does. Her worst suspicions had now been confirmed: Bitter was furtively diverting her fortune to Holland. Luckily she had been notified of this before the last ship of the fleet had weighed anchor, which enabled her to send a last-minute letter to an acquaintance in Holland, asking him to inform the Company directors of Bitter's illicit activities.

On 15 February 1677 a furious Cornelia appealed to the Court of Justice. She accused her husband of stealing her property and of mistreating her. The Governor-General of the Council of the Indies had already given her permission on 22 December to have a summons served on her husband.[19] She demanded a separation, restitution of the 25,000 rixdollars, Bitter's removal from the house, and the return of various slaves who had been freed by their new master against the wishes of their mistress. Most importantly, she petitioned the court to nullify the privileges granted to her husband in the marriage settlement.[20]

Bitter now began collecting all the evidence he could possibly use against Cornelia. He paid a visit to the church council and complained that he had been "cited in *causa divortii* before the Court of Justice." Because this had tarnished his reputation, he asked the council to issue "a declaration concerning his behavior toward his wife."[21]

The church council decided to comply with this request, and provided him with "a historically accurate account of the circumstances in accordance with the church's documents." In the minutes of the meeting of 1 March we find the complete text of the report (*attestatio*) requested by Bitter. A quick perusal of its contents reveals Bitter's motives in asking for it: from the moment the marriage had started to go wrong, Bitter had carefully kept within the bounds of the law, whereas his frustrated wife had given free rein to her emotions.

The report states that Bitter, after being admonished by the church council, had declared himself to be "reasonable and ready for a reconciliation," but that his wife had shown herself, "on the contrary, to be irreconcilable." Bitter had even seriously requested the council members to visit his wife one last time and implore her to make up with him. According to the report, Reverend Zas, together with a colleague and an elder, had gone to the Bitter household on the day after Christmas in an attempt to restore peace and "show their good will." On 2 January, however, Zas reported to his regret that his peace mission had been an utter failure and that Bitter's wife had rejected his proposals "with obstinate implacability after repeated and serious attempts by every means in their power to mollify her high-strung feelings."[22]

Armed with the church's report, Bitter felt strong enough to launch a counteroffensive. He asked the Court of Justice to order Cornelia "to return to her husband and to live in peace and the fear of God."[23] He argued that, quite apart from the marriage settlement, he had the legal right to the guardianship and management of Cornelia's property. In addition, he laid claim to half her income, the interest accruing from it, and usufructuary rights to her fortune.

Tug-of-War with the Church Council

Despite his legally convincing claims, Bitter made little progress because he was such an incorrigible hothead. On 1 April Reverend Zas drew the attention of the honorable members of the church council to a shameful incident. Seven days previously, several members of the Court of Justice—accompanied by the secretary of the Council of the Indies, the bailiff, a certain Miss Judith, and Cornelia herself—had served a summons on Bitter. Taking courage from those in the entourage, Cornelia must have made the bold decision to pay a visit to her house and pick up some of her belongings. During the visit those present clearly heard Bitter say that "Reverend Zas was unworthy of setting foot in the pulpit, uttering many more terms of abuse as well." Reverend Zas took these insults very personally indeed. Was Bitter insinuating that he had chosen Cornelia's side for improper reasons when acting as mediator in their marital dispute? Zas could not let this pass without comment. He made it clear to the church elders that such remarks were insulting not just to him but to the entire church council. Immediate action was called for: the members of the church council decided to launch an investigation. All of Batavia must have enjoyed watching these proceedings, as they degenerated into an operetta-like melodrama that dragged on for nearly a year.

To Zas's dismay, however, it appeared that no one present at the scene of the crime was willing to testify against Bitter. It is possible, of course, that Bitter had only made a joke and that no one had taken him seriously. After a stormy debate, however, one of those present at the scene, Gualter Sleeman, did admit that the statement recorded in the minutes of the meeting held on 1 April was essentially correct, whereupon Bitter was summoned to appear before the church council. He stated that first he "wanted to hear the exact words of the accusation against him and would then be willing to explain his conduct." Bitter was given eight days to produce a written statement. Apparently the old fox was hoping to win time.[24]

It is quite likely that in the following weeks Zas did everything in his power to persuade his colleagues to take action against Bitter, who did not appear again before the council until two and a half months later. When asked why he had failed to come up with a written explanation within one week as promised, he excused himself, saying that he had not yet been able to find any hard evidence and announced his intention to go on searching.[25] Bitter, who realized he could no longer ignore the demands of the church council, now devised another scheme. He wrote a letter to Governor-General Johan Maetsuycker, complaining about the way he was being pestered—persecuted even—by the church council. His appeal made a deep impression. On 21 June a letter from the Governor-General was read aloud to the church council: Maetsuycker advised the pious gentlemen "not to hurry along this work, nor try to deal with it in a week or two." Apparently Bitter was extremely busy at the Court of Justice, and they should not get in his way unnecessarily.

The council capitulated and again gave Bitter eight days to present his evidence. As he no longer saw a means of escape, Bitter handed over—one week later—a bill from notary Keysers which showed several business transactions involving Zas. According to Bitter, this document proved that Zas was conspiring with Cornelia. When the notary was asked if this was true, he denied the allegation. For the third time Bitter was given eight days in which to come up with truly conclusive evidence. The church council had finally lost its patience and decided to put an end to the matter once and for all.

If the gentlemen thought that Bitter's bag of tricks was now empty, they were sorely mistaken. One week later Johan Bitter appeared with empty hands and informed them, to his great regret, that he was unable to provide any written evidence, because he had already handed over what he had to the Court of Justice. The fact was that he had begun legal proceedings against notary Keysers. This forced the church council to impose severe sanctions. First of all, Bitter was required to apologize to the church council for his belligerent behavior, after which he was to beg Reverend Zas for forgiveness, both gentlemen being expected to honor and respect each other in future. Moreover, Bitter was forbidden to attend the Lord's Supper until he had done what was expected of him.[26]

When Bitter was told of this decision on 1 July, he simply shrugged his shoulders. According to Reverend Pays, who had gone with an elder to his house, Bitter had admitted that his challenge to the council to appear "before the Heavenly Tribunal" had been made in haste, and he regretted having said it. For this he would gladly offer his apologies to the council, but he was not willing to beg forgiveness of Reverend Zas. The church council would not let themselves be hoodwinked: they took "no satisfaction at all in his answer."

On 1 November Theophilus Bredius, president of the church council, asked whether the judgment recently handed down by the Court of Justice regarding Bitter's argument with Zas had anything to do with the case pending against Bitter. The answer, amazingly enough, was no.[27] It was decided to send the president and an elder to Bitter's house, to reiterate that the church council was still awaiting his apology.

On 8 November the emissaries reported that Bitter had responded briefly and to the point in writing:

> Having been served a citation by the honorable gentlemen Bredius and Van Dam to comply with the church council's resolution by the following Monday, I hereby reply that I stand by the answer I gave on the twenty-fifth, thanking the honorable gentlemen for the trouble they have taken and recommending that the honorable church council exercise prudence in making its wise decisions. Batavia, 6 November 1677. [Signed] J. Bitter.[28]

The devout gentlemen refused to believe that these were Bitter's last words on the subject, so they asked the sexton to invite him again, but on 25 November it was reported that Bitter had nothing more to say on the matter. The council now gave up all hope and declared him *contumax*, willfully disobedient to their orders. From now on Bitter would be denied all opportunity to defend himself before the church council. This was a stringent measure indeed, but what were the immediate consequences for the obstinate person in question? No one knew the answer to this. All eyes now turned toward heaven, but no answer was forthcoming from that quarter either.

Despite having taken the above-mentioned measure, the church council resolved on 29 November to consider Bitter's case a while longer, appealing to the accused and warning him "of the difficulties in store for him." The church elder Van Dam was willing to act as "the bearer of ill tidings." On 6 December he reported that he had spoken to Bitter, who had promised yet again to supply them with a written statement. Sure enough, on 13 December a grimy, "soiled" epistle finally arrived. Its contents, however, did not appease the church council, as Bitter's reply "had nothing to do with the matter put before him." Yet again, it was decided to consider the case a while longer, and—should the opportunity present itself—to call the recalcitrant lawyer to account.[29]

By 3 January 1678 nothing had happened. Reverend Zas, who had been losing sleep over this matter for more than a year now, could stand it no longer. The whole city began to snigger whenever the Reverend showed himself in public. For no matter how disrespectful it sounds, what could be more fun than an uncouth boor who manages to make fools of the reverend and the entire church council for over a year? The Reverend Theodorus Zas finally asked for an "act of justification." Two weeks later, on 17 January 1678, this clerical act was read aloud to the council.[30]

Let us now take a closer look at the tactics Bitter used to keep the church authorities at bay. Not only did he dissemble and make vague promises, but he began parallel proceedings at the Court of Justice, for he thought that the church council would never be able to enforce its disciplinary measures before the Court of Justice had passed judgment in the same case.[31] To all appearances this overblown farce ultimately caused Reverend Zas and the church council much more trouble than it caused the defendant, as the last lines of the act of justification suggest:

And to this day the above-mentioned Mr. Bitter, although seriously warned time and again by this church council, has not been willing to comply with our judgment and opinions. Thus decreed and approved in the meeting of the church council of the city of Batavia, 17 January 1678.

Apparently it was all the same to Bitter. Acting as though nothing had happened, he tried several months later to exact a statement from the church council saying that his wife had screamed "he'll murder me" when they had counseled her to return home. Bitter's request was understandably ignored.[32]

The bickering between Zas and Bitter reveals much about Bitter's tactics. He was constantly collecting evidence, either for his own defense or for use in attacking his opponents. In Bitter's eyes a court case was one long boxing match consisting of nothing but sly digs, preferably below the belt. Moreover, he did not hesitate to call for help whenever he felt cornered. He manipulated and played for time, dragging out the proceedings until his adversaries finally lost heart.

Social control, in the form of disciplinary measures imposed by the church, was one of the cornerstones of Dutch society both at home and abroad. Yet the Protestant church in the Indies, having developed under conditions peculiar to colonial society, was nowhere near as powerful as its Calvinist sister institution in Holland. The church council in Batavia was in effect subordinate to the Governor-General, who, whenever the occasion arose, wrote letters to the pious brothers on the council urging them to come to their senses. A Company employee could ignore the church's orders completely if he felt certain of the support of his superiors, which is why Bitter emerged practically unscathed from his protracted struggle with the church authorities. The only punishment he was really afraid of was disciplinary action imposed by his immediate superiors on the Council of the Indies.

The Strong Arm of the Law

There was, however, one thing that continued to torment Johan Bitter: because he had no inventory at his disposal, he had not succeeded in laying his hands on all of Cornelia's property. Even worse, he had the feeling that she was secretly transferring funds to other people's accounts. His suspicions were confirmed by one case in particular: Cornelia had succeeded in persuading a good friend, Adriaen van Becom, to transfer 3,000 rixdollars, which had previously been deposited with the Company in Cornelia's name, to his own account. At the bottom of the receipt written by the Company cashier, Baukes, Van Becom had written a note saying that the money did not belong to him but to "Mistress Cnoll." He left the receipt with Baukes, who in turn gave it to Cornelia.[33] When Cornelia had begun quarreling with Bitter, she needed money to live on, and Baukes—without Van Becom's knowledge—had secretly given her this money on orders from the Director-General, Rijckloff van Goens, who had been a close friend of the late Pieter Cnoll.

When Bitter found out about the 3,000 rixdollars belonging to Cornelia deposited in Van Becom's name, he had the latter's possessions seized. The Court of Justice ordered Van Becom to pay the money to Bitter and fined him an additional 50 rixdollars. The defendant was understandably offended by this ruling and asked the Governor-General and the Council of the Indies to reconsider the matter, so that every aspect of the case that had not yet surfaced could now be disclosed. "Even though [they] thought that this ruling could not be upheld, since one could perceive in it a manifest inequity," several members of the High Government continued to urge Van Becom to withdraw his request for a review of the case. These gentlemen, of course, had their own reasons for doing so. Rijckloff van Goens, whose actions had been well meant but not strictly lawful, had meanwhile been appointed Governor-General, and he therefore wished to hush up the entire matter. At the same time, they assumed that Bitter did not want the general public to find out that his wife had outwitted him: "As far as Bitter is concerned, he is fearful, and would rather be triumphant in name only than expose himself to the uncertainties of judicial review." Rijckloff van Goens therefore asked Van Becom to waive his request for a review, in exchange for which he was prepared never to carry out the sentence. At long last Van Becom capitulated, informing Johan Bitter that he would not press for a review if he received a written statement guaranteeing that the sentence in question would never be carried out. A secret meeting was arranged in the neighborhood of the Malay Church, and the document was handed over in the presence of Willem van Outhoorn, a member of the Council of the Indies.[34]

The brains behind this operation had been another member of the Council, Cornelis Speelman, who had previously acted as mediator between Johan and Cornelia. This long-standing acquaintance of Cornelia—for many years he had been Pieter Cnoll's superior in the bookkeeping department—was certainly no gentleman in his private life,[35] and perhaps this made him the right person to deal with the wily Bitter, who was terrified of him. This was thoroughly in keeping with François Valentijn's characterization of Speelman: "He was a man who radiated fire and wit, was uncommonly forthright in his speech, wielded great authority, and was generally so feared that everyone trembled in his presence. Yet he was a great champion of his friends."[36]

Years later, after Speelman's death, Bitter would voice his resentment at having been forced by an "old windbag" to forsake his personal interests "out of fear of a man who possessed neither rank nor power."[37] This description was far from accurate: Speelman had plenty of rank and power, having succeeded Van Goens as Director-General. Of more importance is one thing that Bitter failed to mention: at the beginning of 1679, when the understanding had been reached with Van Becom, Bitter's own position in Batavia had become extremely precarious. The trump card that Cornelia had played against him in Holland had begun to turn the game in her favor.

CHAPTER SIX

The Parrot's Account

In the minutes of the proceedings of the Amsterdam Chamber of the Dutch East India Company we find, in the entry for 29 July 1677, the first reference to the little bag of diamonds that Bitter had sent in secret to Holland. The second mate of the homeward-bound ship *Europa*, a character with the implausible name of Jan Hay (Jack Shark), appeared on that Tuesday morning before the Amsterdam directors and was interrogated by Messrs. Tulp, Van Loon, Backer, and Graaflant. The Company's lawyer, Pieter van Dam, who had traveled from The Hague to Amsterdam for the occasion, was present as well. Hay produced a cloth bag containing the twenty-four diamonds that Johan Bitter had entrusted to him in Batavia. A notary, who had been summoned to record Hay's testimony, noted that their combined value was estimated at 8,000 guilders. Hay, for his part, could not tell his interlocutors where the precious stones had come from, though he did say—in exchange for a promise that no charges would be pressed against him if he cooperated in their investigation—that there must be a number of letters and a bill of lading which could supply them with more information. Just where these letters were, though, he could not say.[1] The mystery was solved two weeks later, when Isaac Hochepied—the director who had confiscated the "little bag of diamonds" at Texel harbor—handed over to the investigating committee a personal letter from

Bitter, along with a stack of letters addressed to other persons.[2]

The gentlemen were in for a big surprise. Among the letters, in which Bitter told of his arrival in Batavia and bragged about the big fish he had landed there, they found a bill of exchange issued by the Batavian alderman Jacob Does. It was addressed to the Amsterdam merchant Pieter van Wicquevoort, giving him the right to have the Company treasurer cash it for 3,000 rixdollars. The letters, however, made it clear that the money was not from Does but from Bitter. A complete inventory giving the weight, number, and value of the diamonds was found in a letter addressed to another merchant in Amsterdam.

The minutes of the meeting of 8 September 1677 reveal that Bitter "expected to be sent a receipt [for the diamonds and the bill of exchange] made out to another name, apparently for fear of the truth being brought to light." Another letter, addressed to Isaacq Staets, left little room for doubt as to Bitter's actual intentions: he apologized for not being in a position to send from Batavia the "curiosities" that Staets had requested.[3] The Amsterdam directors, extremely vexed because this letter seemed to confirm their original suspicions about Bitter's involvement in private trade, reported on their findings at the next general meeting of the Heren XVII. They proposed recalling the culprit immediately and demoting him without pay.[4]

The directors were angry with Bitter for reasons that had as little to do with the divorce case as with his wife's money. They were dismayed to find out that one of their qualified personnel—who had been appointed by them and had a seat on the Court of Justice no less—had been caught smuggling diamonds, and they were afraid that a great deal of illegally acquired money was being sent without their knowledge from the Indies to Holland in the form of gems.[5]

In the *Papegaey* ("Parrot Book")—a legal form book containing "all manner of petitions, charges, conclusions, and so on, serving in daily practice the various Courts of Holland"—we find the text of a petition submitted by the Company in 1675 to the Court of Holland regarding a clear-cut case of diamond smuggling.[6] The case had come to the attention of the Company's directors because the parties involved had contested the rightful ownership of the gems and had been foolish enough to ask the Court to mediate in the dispute. When the Company got wind of this, it did not hesitate to demand that all evidence be produced in court. Because the diamonds had been imported illegally, the request had been granted.[7] Perhaps Bitter was not aware of this smuggling case, since the verdict had been delivered shortly after he had left Holland for the Indies. This precedent proves, however, that the Company saw to it that the ban on the diamond trade was strictly upheld.

Early in 1677 the smuggling case involving Bitter figured prominently on the agenda of the general meeting of the Heren XVII.[8] The Amsterdam Chamber had prepared the case so well that it could be dealt with in only one morning. The diamonds were confiscated according to Article 23 of the terms of employment that all Company employees, including Bitter, were required to sign. At the same time it was decided to withhold for the time being payment to Van Wicquevoort of the 3,000 guilders stipulated in the bill of exchange. The total value of the bag of diamonds and the bill of exchange was estimated at 16,450 guilders.

The Heren XVII decided to write to Governor-General Maetsuycker, requesting him to urge the Court of Justice at Batavia to take decisive action in this case. Perhaps severe punishment would serve as a warning to others. All of Bitter's letters were therefore sent back to the Indies to be used as evidence. At the end of their epistle the directors added a curious note to the effect that "no matter what judgment was passed in the case" the previously mentioned lawyer Johan Bitter "should be sent home without delay as an employee useless to the Company."[9] This time the Heren XVII quickly agreed that Bitter should be dealt with mercilessly.

The Punishment

On 6 June 1678 the East Indiamen *China* and *Land van Schouwen* dropped anchor at Batavia, after a voyage lasting nine months and nineteen days. That same afternoon the letters sent by the Heren XVII were quickly given a first reading in Batavia Castle, resulting in Bitter's being summoned directly from his office in the town hall. Upon appearing at the Castle, he was charged with illegal trading in diamonds and dismissed from his post on the spot.[10] It is not clear how he attempted to account for his actions during the following months, though it is certain that he was now involved in two lawsuits: one in which he was charged with smuggling diamonds and the other involving his separation from Cornelia, which had already been going on for some time. From the documents it emerges that Bitter had been forced to borrow a small fortune: 4,300 rixdollars, to be exact. He had presumably been compelled to do so because the court had forbidden him, pending the divorce case, to draw on either the joint household account or Cornelia's capital. One week before the ruling, however, he had secretly managed to obtain a mortgage on Cornelia's house from the alderman Jacob Does, the same man who had transferred to Amsterdam Bitter's bill of exchange for 3,000 rixdollars.[11]

The divorce proceedings took place under strange circumstances. Several members of the Court declared themselves either unwilling or unable to pass judgment in the case. As Bitter's friends and colleagues, they considered themselves too personally involved in the matter to be able to form an objective opinion and asked to be replaced by impartial outsiders. Owing in part to this development, a member of the Council of the Indies, Dirk Blom, was appointed to the Court of Justice and charged with the special task of expediting the settlement of several lawsuits that were being delayed or even willfully obstructed.[12]

By now everyone in Batavia knew that the Heren XVII were out to get Bitter. Realizing that he was cornered and therefore all the more desperate, the special court decided to punish the arrogant newcomer from Holland who had so ineptly tried to rob Cornelia of her fortune. Because "there was no prospect of their ever being reconciled and reunited," Cornelia's request for a separation was tentatively granted on 4 November 1679.

Cornelia could not have expected more under the circumstances. Such separations were in theory only temporary; the judge was allowed to grant a separation only with the understanding that there was hope of reconciliation.[13] Luckily for Cornelia, the decision had other ramifications. The defendant was denied all the privileges laid down in the marriage settlement: he was required not only to pay back the 25,000 rixdollars but also to give back the house and several slaves whom he had meanwhile freed. He also had to pay all legal costs.[14] The judgment handed down by the court was grist to the church council's mill. Two days later the council issued a warning to Bitter, urging him to reflect on his actions and to pay closer attention to the fulfillment of his Christian duties.[15]

The verdict in the diamond smuggling case was issued a week later, on 11 November 1679. Bitter was found guilty, dismissed from his post, and ordered to return home:

> Considering that a decision was handed down by the Court of Justice several days ago in the case involving the Honorable Johan Bitter, former member of the Court of Justice, and his wife Cornelia van Nijenroode, granting her a legal separation, it has been agreed, based on the order of the Right Honorable Gentlemen (the Heren XVII), to have him repatriated.[16]

Bitter had defended himself by saying "that he had sent some diamonds to Holland to have a few pieces of jewelry made there for his daughters," but his plea had not been taken seriously.[17]

In a last desperate attempt to thwart the goddess of vengeance, two

months later, on 2 January 1680, Bitter addressed himself directly to
the High Government and requested a review of the ruling given in the
divorce case in Batavia (which would of course mean a delay in his
repatriation to Holland). If this was not granted, he would request a
court order requiring his wife to accompany him on his return trip. This
second request was especially cunning, for what chance did Cornelia
have in Holland, where she knew absolutely no one, to defend herself
against her husband with all his Amsterdam patrons?

Both requests were denied, though Bitter was informed that, upon
arrival in the Netherlands, he could appeal to any court he wished.
Bitter submitted "further elucidation" to his request, but to no avail.
The authorities held firm and advised him to reread the terse instructions they had sent him on 19 December. He was being sent back to
Holland by the Heren XVII as an "employee useless to the Company
and was hereby ordered, in accordance with the decision of the Right
Honorable Gentlemen, to sail with the last homeward-bound ship of
the season, being further advised to seek advice in Holland."[18] The
church authorities proved to be more biddable. At his request, Bitter
was given copies of all the resolutions concerning his marital problems,
though he was sensible enough not to ask for the documents referring
to his conflict with Reverend Zas.

Just before his departure another problem arose. Jacob Does and
Mattheus Luchtenburgh, the two men from whom Bitter had borrowed
considerable sums of money in recent months, requested that Johan
Bitter be held in custody until he had paid his debts. Their request was
denied, however.[19]

The journal kept at Batavia Castle records that at dawn on 15
March 1680 the homeward-bound ships 't Huijs te Merwe and Ternate
set sail "for the harbors of our beloved fatherland . . . may the Lord God
grant them a safe journey."[20]

Aboard the Ternate, whose captain was Willem Kemp, there were, in
addition to 122 sailors and 29 soldiers, three women, one child, and

two "unemployed people." The latter were Johan Bitter and his servant. When the fleet had set sail—by evening the ships were visible only as dots on the horizon—Cornelia van Nijenroode must have breathed a sigh of relief, having been released from her tormentor at long last.

During the long voyage of the homeward-bound *Ternate*, Johan Bitter had more than enough time to ponder his fate. He worried about the reception he would receive from the Heren XVII and brooded over his chances of ultimately defeating Cornelia. He was convinced that the Company directors, frequently confronted with diamond smuggling in the past, would react skeptically to the plea that he had given the gems to Jan Hay to have them made into jewelry for his daughters. If he wanted to win this case, he would once again need the protection of his patron Gillis Valckenier. Bitter realized that this time it would be useless to scheme in advance. He would just have to bide his time until he arrived in Holland.

But it was not in Bitter's nature to sit around twiddling his thumbs. There was nothing stopping him from appealing to the Court of Holland and instituting legal proceedings against his headstrong wife, assuming that the court had the authority to pass judgment in such cases. Here was a possible loophole: on the basis of the provisional separation it could be verified that the defendant, Cornelia, was living in the East Indies, and because the Court of Holland had no jurisdiction there, it did not have the power to deal with any legal action taken against her. After mulling things over for a long time, the lawyer thought he had found his own solution to the problem.

Bad news was awaiting Bitter upon his arrival in Amsterdam: his powerful patron, Gillis Valckenier, had died. This was a nasty blow, but luckily there were still a few members of the board of the Amsterdam Chamber—Louis Trip and Dirck Tulp, for example—who were inclined to think well of him, and presumably they gave Bitter some useful advice and support.

He was told, for example, that the Company directors were considering a change of course as regards their attitude toward the diamond trade. The Heren XVII realized that this was an evil that could not be eradicated by the adoption of punitive measures. Perhaps the only solution was to legalize it. The Company itself did not trade in diamonds, but perhaps it should permit its employees to engage in the diamond trade under certain specified conditions. There were endless discussions about how the matter should be dealt with. This unexpected turn of events increased Bitter's chances of winning the war, and he therefore thought it best to keep quiet until the board had made a decision.

But in his suit against Cornelia pending at the Court of Holland Bitter did not want to waste any time, and he therefore decided to perform some legal legerdemain in order to demonstrate the Court's jurisdiction in this case. Bitter attempted to prove the judge's competence to pass judgment by requesting a writ of sequestration. This was an order authorizing the bailiff to seize everything belonging to Cornelia that was deposited with the Company, including all goods, charters (written agreements), and papers deposited with the Amsterdam Chamber. By means of this writ, the Company (which fell under the Court of Holland's jurisdiction) became involved, willy-nilly, in the fight between Bitter and Cornelia. The Court's power to pass judgment in lawsuits involving the Dutch East India Company automatically gave it the power to pass judgment in the legal proceedings against Cornelia. And so, probably in January 1681, though the exact date is not known, Bitter petitioned the Court of Holland to have Cornelia's possessions seized. This was his opening move in a new attempt to checkmate the "iron butterfly" in Batavia.

Thanks to Willem van Alphen, whose "Parrot Book" has already supplied us with valuable information about the illegal trade in diamonds, we may reconstruct the chain of events leading up to the sequestration.[21] Luckily, the "Parrot Book" contains not only the text of the petition, but also more important documents relating to the formal side of the case and the judgment that was eventually handed down.

The purpose of Bitter's petition was twofold: to obtain a writ of sequestration, thereby safeguarding his claims against Cornelia, and to force an opening to a new round in his fight against his obstinate wife. The main points of the petition clearly show that the lawyer Bitter was in his element.

Bitter declared that he, a widower, had married Cornelia van Nijenroode—"born in Hirado in Japan, at the time [of their marriage] widow of Pieter Cnoll"—in March 1676 under the terms of a marriage settlement. He was not entitled to community property, though several conditions had been stipulated in the agreement, including preferential treatment for the surviving spouse. After the marriage had been solemnized, he had behaved like "a pious, honest, decent, and peace-loving man." His wife, however, had been prompted by others to provoke a quarrel over the administration of her property and the investment of "certain monies." Despite the law that gave him, the guardian, the right to deal with these matters as he saw fit, he had assented to signing an agreement aimed at avoiding future quarrels and designed to create an atmosphere of cooperation and affection. He had even consented to having his children board with other families, "at great expense," because their stepmother would not tolerate their presence in her house.

Unfortunately, none of these measures had helped. His wife had only stirred up new quarrels and had eventually left the house, "separating herself on her own authority from her husband." She had turned a deaf ear to the church council's exhortations to seek a reconciliation with her husband and had even ordered her slaves and household servants not to obey him. Moreover, she was secretly diverting her funds elsewhere and having her possessions removed from the house. She had falsely accused him of abusing her (Bitter was referring, of course, to the incident involving the dislocated shoulder) and had finally instituted legal proceedings against him. In February 1677 she had demanded a separation, and—Bitter made a point of emphasizing—through the intervention of people who were not qualified to pass judgment, the Court had come to a tentative decision on 4 November 1679 that was completely in her favor: a separation coupled with an injunction forbidding her husband to exert control over her property.

After stating the facts, Bitter arrived at the petition proper. He noted that "in various respects the judgment handed down was null and void" and pointed out that a temporary separation was not the same as a definite divorce. He maintained that the marriage had not foundered owing to desertion or adultery on his part; the nuptial bonds had not been broken and the separation was therefore only a temporary one. He went on to say that his attempts to take his wife with him to Holland on the same ship—or another one, if she did not wish to travel with him—had been intentionally thwarted. The authorities in Batavia had ordered him to leave immediately, adding that if he could not acquiesce in their decision, he would have to seek redress in Holland. This meant, in his opinion, that the jurisdiction of the Court was based on the place of residence of the petitioner and not, as was usually the case, on that of the defendant. In short, the plaintiff had followed the advice given him by the authorities in Batavia, which meant that his current place of residence fell under the jurisdiction of the Court of Holland.

To lend more weight to his argument, Bitter claimed that his wife's stubborn perseverance in this matter was unchristian and should not be tolerated by a Christian authority, especially as he, the plaintiff, was prepared to do anything to bring about a reconciliation and live together with his wife in peace and harmony. He could not recall that he had ever insulted her; on the contrary, he only wanted to love her as befitted any God-fearing, Christian husband.

With respect to the jurisdiction of the Court—the Achilles heel in this case—Bitter asserted that his wife's place of residence should not be seen as different from his own. He therefore humbly beseeched the

Court to issue a writ of sequestration directing the bailiff to seize all goods, charters, papers, and other effects that could be demonstrated to belong to Cornelia van Nijenroode. This also affected all persons in the possession of property actually belonging to Cornelia. Finally, he implored the Court to order Cornelia to effect a reconciliation with her husband, return to their household, and live with him as a good Christian wife should, "till death do them part." The plaintiff, in turn, undertook—as a Christian and peace-loving husband—to love his wife and fulfill his obligations, though he asked the Court to declare his wife a "malicious deserter" if she refused to seek a reconciliation. In that case she would forfeit all the advantages enumerated in the marriage settlement. He, the plaintiff, would then be entitled to the advantages that would accrue to him in the event of his wife's death. Bitter also made an attempt to remedy his abysmal financial situation: pending the suit, he requested an "adequate portion of the income" arising from the goods that had been seized.

The sequestration that took place on 26 February 1681 proves that the Court did indeed issue the writ. Cornelia herself (or a proxy) was summoned to appear before the Court at The Hague on the first Monday of October 1682. This date, so far in the future, clearly shows that the Court had taken into account the time necessary to serve a summons on Cornelia in Batavia.[22]

Five Angry Men

Yet another document relating to this case was published by Van Alphen in the "Parrot Book." It is a "consultation," or legal advice regarding the marriage settlement between Bitter and his bride. This document, drawn up by five lawyers on 21 February 1681, is dated five days earlier than the writ of sequestration. Is it possible that the Court of Holland, confused by Bitter's request, felt compelled to seek advice before coming to a decision? This is almost inconceivable. A sequestration carried out to safeguard one's claims, such as that ordered here, does not create problems as long as the claim is, on the face of it, legitimate. Bitter's request met this requirement. The fact that his petition was given a hearing, however, did not automatically mean that sequestration was justified. A decision to this effect could be arrived at only after the Court had given the matter considerable thought. For this reason, issuing a writ of sequestration was a routine matter, and it was usually done swiftly to prevent the goods in question from disappearing beforehand. It would therefore have been highly unusual for the Court to find itself in such a dilemma that it could not pass judgment without first seeking the opinion of five legal advisers. It seems more likely that this document was drawn up to underscore Bitter's arguments. The ever anticipatory lawyer was, after all, extraordinarily adept at devising and presenting "evidence" of this kind.

At the beginning of the consultation the advisers reviewed the documents put before them. They took note, among other things, of the marriage settlement, the "cohabitation contract" designed "to avoid all foreseeable troubles," and the evidence presented at the hearing in Batavia, including the Court's decision to grant a separation. They judged Bitter to be attentive and diligent in his work, to have an agreeable, polite, and easy-going manner, and to be open to the idea of reconciliation. All this was presented as being in stark contrast to his shrewish wife. The testimony betrays the hand of a skillful manipulator. It emerges from this consultation that the advisers were keenly aware of Bitter's fears that he could not expect just treatment in the Indies. Clearly, a file like this could only have been compiled by Bitter himself.

It is therefore hardly surprising that the advisers wanted to put some pressure on the Court of Justice at Batavia, where Bitter had supposedly received such unjust treatment. This Court had been "deliberately misleading" when it had maintained that Bitter had no right to his wife's income and the interest accruing from her assets because the marriage settlement had denied him community property. The Court should have realized that all such profit yielded by the spouse's assets "are and will remain community property." According to the law, the husband was entitled to manage all the assets, even those that his wife had withheld from joint ownership. Disregarding for the time being the question of whether the separation had been granted on justifiable grounds, the lawyers nevertheless thought that Bitter had been put at a serious disadvantage by the decision requiring him to give everything back to his wife and to bear the high cost of supporting his children, who had been forced to board with other families.

If his wife were to terminate the marriage settlement unilaterally, then she would have to pay compensation to her husband. The counselors also established that the Court of Justice had permitted a member of the court, who had testified under oath in the case in question, to participate in the decision. (They were probably referring to Cornelis Speelman.) Furthermore, Bitter's request to bring about a reconciliation had been rejected, even though it was the duty of every judge to attempt *ex officiis* to effect a reconciliation.[23]

The advisers were unsparing in their censure of the Batavian Court of Justice. Even the High Government of the Dutch Indies did not escape their devastating criticism. Bitter had been dishonored by the order to return to Holland without his wife and children while the case in which reconciliation seemed a real possibility was still under consideration. Neither had he been given a chance to request a review of the case. The advisers ignored the plea that the Batavian High Government had acted in this way because it dared not ignore the order issued by the Heren XVII to repatriate Bitter. They consequently concluded that in this way a man "of agreeable, pleasant manner, good and modest in his ways" had become the victim of derailed legal action.

Up to here the consultation was closely linked to the content of Bitter's petition and provided, moreover, welcome support to his claims. On the face of it, the lawyers were right in finding that Bitter had been unjustly treated. The surprising part, however, is that they made no mention in their concluding statements of Bitter's petition, leaving unresolved the question of whether his claims were indeed admissible in a Dutch court. Perhaps they were in doubt on this matter. They advised Bitter, who had been badly treated in the Indies, to turn to the highest authority in the land: the States General. This body had the power to mediate in all cases involving people who thought they had received unfair treatment before the law in the Indies.[24]

Reading between the lines of this advice, Bitter knew that the learned gentlemen had little faith that a petition for a review of the judgment handed down in Batavia would be honored by the Court of Holland. Was this why he had carefully avoided using the word "review" in his petition?

The Sequestration

On 27 February 1681 the first bailiff of the Hague Chamber of the Court of Holland betook himself, bailiff's staff in hand, to the Plein in The Hague. There he knocked on the door of the hostelry of the Dutch East India Company, where the members of the Hague Besoigne, the Company's executive committee, were meeting. At the request of Johan Bitter, former member of the Court of Justice in the Indies, and in the name of the authorities, the bailiff, in the presence of the assembled gentlemen, seized the sum of 34,000 rixdollars, which had been deposited in the Company's treasury by Cornelia van Nijenroode, and additional capital amounting to 12,000 rixdollars deposited by Bitter. Moreover, he laid claims to all other funds and all the property that Cornelia might have deposited with the Company without his knowledge, including all the accrued interest—past, present, and future. The bailiff ordered the board of directors to "accept and comply with" the writ of sequestration. He summoned Cornelia van Nijenroode to appear before the Court on the first Monday of the month of October 1682, at the same time handing over copies of the writ and the accompanying document.

Pieter van Dam, a Company lawyer known from his masterly *Beschrijvinge*[25]—a handbook, reserved for the exclusive use of the Heren XVII, which described the organization and management of the Dutch East India Company—received the unexpected visitor. He accepted the bailiff's documents, saying only, "We take notice of the order and will carry it out." The bailiff then took his leave, and the members of the Besoigne, shaking their heads, went back to discussing more important matters. Bitter, with his penchant for legal wrangling, had lost none of his old ways. Little did they know that this was only the beginning of a long-drawn-out story that would eventually take up a great deal of their valuable time.[26]

Two weeks later another bailiff paid a similar visit to two residents of Amsterdam, Nicolaes de Roy and Gijsbrecht David Strantwijck. Bitter suspected that both gentlemen were in the possession of documents, deeds, and other property belonging to Cornelia. The bailiff appeared to be at the wrong address in the case of Strantwijck, for the latter said curtly, "I have no such papers." De Roy, however, answered, "Yes, it is true," and admitted to having power of attorney to act on Cornelia's behalf.[27]

After carrying out these orders to the best of his ability, it was time for the bailiff to inform Cornelia of the writ of sequestration and to serve a summons on her. Because Cornelia was living in Batavia, the bailiff, again at Bitter's request, did this by means of an edict issued on 14 March 1681 at The Hague.[28] First of all, the bells of the Hague town hall were rung, after which the writ "by public edict" was read from the front steps, ordering Cornelia to assent to the sequestration and forbidding her to do anything to obstruct it. She was also instructed to seek reconciliation and return to her husband's side. Finally, she was sum-

moned to appear before the Court, in person or by proxy, on the first
Monday of the month of October 1682. The bailiff put the text of the
edict in a missive addressed to Cornelia van Nijenroode, which also
contained copies of the writ of sequestration and the summons. It was
now Nicolaes de Roy's task to ensure that the letter was handed over
to Cornelia at the first possible opportunity.

Once he had set the wheels of justice in motion, all Bitter could do
was sit back and speculate about further developments, extremely satisfied with what he had achieved so far. But would his attempt to cir-
cumvent Batavia's judgment succeed? And would Cornelia's actions
provide him with an opportunity to brand her a "malicious deserter,"
with all the financial advantages that would be his as a result? He could
not imagine her *not* fighting back. Sooner or later the marriage would
fall apart again; it was only a matter of time. If his darkest scenario
came true and his petition was declared null and void, the only course
open to him would be to request a review of his case in Batavia. But
returning to Batavia would only be possible if the charges of diamond
smuggling were dropped. The outcome was now in the hands of fate.

CHAPTER SEVEN

The Lost Sheep

In the meantime, in far-off Batavia, Cornelia van Nijenroode was completely unaware of the latest developments. She had been granted a temporary separation, her husband had been dismissed from his post and sent back to Holland, and he had failed in his attempt to take her along with him. Cornelia had every reason to feel relieved, even though she worried about the possible legal ramifications of the huge amounts of money that Bitter had borrowed shortly before his departure for Holland.[1] It seemed, however, that she had been freed of her tormentor for good, and she looked forward to the future with a light heart. After all, justice was on her side. Her financial losses were not inconsiderable, but she had enough money in hand to take part in Batavia's expensive social life, which she had reluctantly forgone in recent years because of her quarrels with Bitter. When the rainy season was over, Cornelia had the horses hitched up to the carriage, determined to make trips through the countryside as she had once done.

But the pleasure she took in these little jaunts was short-lived. Dismayed by the decadent behavior of the Batavian burghers, the authorities had decided years before that luxury, "like the plague, should be eradicated in Batavia and the whole of the Indies by means of rules and regulations."[2] With somber regularity all manner of ordinances were issued regarding the display of pomp; this time it was a general ban on the possession of "coaches or covered calashes."³ Only the Governor-General and members of the Council of the Indies were still permitted to ride in carriages, and so the wheels of Cornelia's status symbol slowly ground to a halt.

Nevertheless, Cornelia gradually recovered her former gaiety. The higher circles of society at the Castle welcomed her back, and invitations started to pour in. Encouraged by these developments she sent, at the end of June 1680, a letter to the church council asking for permission to be included again among the communicants at the Lord's Supper.⁴ The deacons did not immediately deny her request, but first they expected Mistress Van Nijenroode to reveal to them her true feelings as regards her absent spouse. The church council suggested she take a more lenient attitude toward him.

Married couples living in discord were not, on principle, supposed to attend the Lord's Supper. This is what prompted the honorable gentlemen to inquire about the exact conditions of the separation. In July Cornelia was not yet among the communicants. Refusing to accept defeat, she paid a visit—before the next meeting at which new candidates would be reviewed—to an old acquaintance, the honorable Theodorus Zas, and asked if he would put in a good word for her. Even the good Reverend Zas was unable to help her, however, and again her request was denied.⁵

Being barred from the Lord's Supper meant that Cornelia could not participate as a full member of the Christian community, but this did not prevent her from attending many important social events. When Petronella Wonderaer, wife of Director-General Cornelis Speelman, died in 1681, Cornelia was present to accept condolences on behalf of her old friend,⁶ and the next day she went to Petronella's house to help receive the mourners after the funeral.

A year later the church council finally pronounced the *nihil obstat* in Cornelia's case. At the request of the church council, Cornelia declared that there was, theoretically, nothing standing in the way of a reconciliation with her husband, should the opportunity present itself.[7] If only she had known what her husband had been doing in the meantime to effect such a reconciliation, she would probably have preferred not to attend the Lord's Supper. In Batavia, however, "forgive and forget" seemed to be the watchword. The lost sheep had returned to the fold.

A Letter from Holland

At the beginning of November 1681 Willem van Outhoorn, president of the Court of Justice at Batavia, summoned its members to a special meeting. After welcoming the gentlemen, he went on to explain why he had called them together. A couple of days after the arrival of the fleet from Holland, Jan Blieck had paid him a visit, informing him that he had the power of attorney to deliver a letter from the bailiff of the Court of Holland to Johan Bitter's wife. One glance at the document was enough to alert Van Outhoorn to the danger: this was a matter to be dealt with at a plenary session. Blieck, who had been waiting in the hall, was called in to hand over the document addressed to Cornelia van Nijenroode, as well as a short letter from Bitter in which he requested the Court of Justice to have the sealed missive delivered to his wife by the local bailiff. Bitter's request seemed reasonable, but the gentlemen on the Batavian Court were not inclined to lend their former colleague a helping hand. Clearly fed up, they told Bitter's representative to deliver the letter himself. Knowing Cornelia, Blieck realized this was more easily said than done.[8]

After some consultation, Blieck called in the help of a local notary, Christoffel van Outgers, who said he would go to Cornelia and give her the letter personally. A few days later he returned with the letter still in his hands; he had not even succeeded in speaking to her. Unwilling to lose more time, Blieck asked the notary to hand over the letter to one of the servants in the Bitter household, and, if they refused to accept it, to leave the letter on the doorstep. In Holland a writ of sequestration would have been nailed to the front door, but the front porch of a Batavian house made it necessary to take a different tack, and this, as we shall see, had less satisfactory results.

When the unfortunate notary arrived at the house on Tiger Canal, he was met at the entrance by the same slave girl he had spoken to before. When asked if the lady of the house or her son were at home, she retorted with a brusque "no." Van Outgers then asked the girl if she would please give her mistress the letter he had brought and explained again what was in the envelope, upon which the girl said, "I'm not allowed to accept any documents." By now the notary realized he would have to resort to leaving the letter on a chair on the front porch. "You can't do that," screamed the girl, "I'll throw it out on the street." Van Outgers, who was no match for this spitfire, beat a hasty retreat, but not without protesting about "all the expense and the damages involved." Looking back over his shoulder from a safe distance, he saw the girl hurl the papers into the street. The punctilious notary made a detailed report of it all, which is recorded in the "Parrot Book."[9] The church council, ever vigilant in matters concerning the well-being and behavior of its flock, seized this opportunity to exercise its pastoral authority. The gentlemen did not hesitate to voice their disapproval of the behavior of this lady, who, only six months before, had shown such a repentant attitude toward her husband that she had been allowed once more to attend the Lord's Supper. Petrus Wijtens, the diligent deputy secretary, was asked to make a certified copy of the promise Cornelia had made in writing the previous July, so that Johan Bitter would be able to take cognizance of the fact in Holland.[10]

Cornelia van Nijenroode, feeling cornered, could no longer ignore the proceedings instigated against her and formally accepted the writ of sequestration issued at The Hague. She must have been terrified at the prospect of a lawsuit in Holland, a country completely unknown to her where she could not count on anyone's help, unlike her cunning husband with all his friends in legal circles. The mere thought of her case being handled by judges who had no insight into social conditions in Batavia was enough to strike fear into her heart. She had no choice but to find a lawyer and appointed—probably through connections in Holland—the Hague lawyer Adriaen van Sterrevelt to act on her behalf at the Court of Holland.

Bitter's Claim

Less than a year later, on the first Monday in October 1682, the case was actually brought before the court at The Hague. Adriaen van Sterrevelt acted on Cornelia's behalf, with George Roosenboom defending Johan Bitter and Cornelis Vinck representing the Dutch East India Company. At the request of the claimant, who was probably seeking assurances that his wife would not be allowed to wriggle her way out of an unfavorable ruling, the defendant declared herself willing to obey the judgment passed by the Court, whereupon both parties made their opening statements.[11]

As was to be expected, Roosenboom's statement closely followed the text of the "Request for a Writ of Sequestration," though one point had been elaborated upon. The original claim stated that, should Cornelia be declared a "malicious deserter," the terms of their divorce would be based on community property. Bitter's lawyer now went one step further, claiming that the husband should have a right not only to half their joint property but also, as a punishment to Cornelia, to a quarter of her half.

The concise statement presented by Cornelia's lawyer, Van Sterrevelt, was based on purely formal grounds: Bitter's claims were not admissible in Court because the case had already been decided by the Court of Justice at Batavia, whose judgment was binding. Such a plea, claiming that the subject matter of a lawsuit has been dealt with and determined in a previous suit, is called an *exceptio rei judicatae*.

On behalf of the Dutch East India Company, Vinck declared that it was probably not possible to prove whether Cornelia had money or goods deposited with a Chamber of the Company in the Dutch Republic and that such assets deposited in the Indies were not subject to sequestration. The case then proceeded as usual. Van Sterrevelt pleaded *exceptio* and the Court withdrew for deliberation.

Judgment was handed down on 22 December 1682. The sequestration was allowed, inasmuch as it concerned Bitter's attempt to effect a reconciliation, with respect to which Van Sterrevelt's *exceptio* was rejected. On all the other points, however, Bitter's claims were declared inadmissible and unjustified owing to the binding nature of the judgment handed down in Batavia.[12] The succinct wording of the judgment and the Court's willingness to accept, at least partially, the *exceptio*, suggest that the gentlemen on the bench were extremely reluctant to open up a Pandora's box of Batavian troubles.

Van Sterrevelt had done his best, achieving all that could be expected. His client could be satisfied with his performance. Cornelia's lawyer must have been aware that a serious attempt at reconciliation could not be blocked. For Bitter this setback had far-reaching consequences: now he had no hope of circumventing the judgment passed in Batavia and triumphing over Cornelia in Holland. The only course open to him, therefore, was to reopen the case in Batavia.

Was Bitter surprised at the judgment handed down by the Court of Holland? Apparently not, because months before the case came up he was already making preparations to request a review of the judgment passed by the Court of Justice at Batavia. In the meantime, his position with respect to the Heren XVII had changed dramatically. For one thing, the bills of exchange that Bitter had sent from Batavia had meanwhile been cleared. Because they had been accepted by the cashier of Batavia Castle, the Company directors were forced to admit that there were no legal grounds on which to block their payment in

Holland. Quite unexpectedly, a sizable sum of money fell into Bitter's lap, enabling him to pay off his debts. Now the most important thing was to have the charge of smuggling dropped. The Heren XVII were discovering that it was not so easy to disprove Bitter's claim that he had sent the diamonds to Holland to have them made into jewelry for his daughters.

On 15 June 1682 an important meeting was held regarding the conditions under which the diamond trade might be legalized. It was suggested that anyone wishing to send diamonds from the Orient to the Netherlands should in future be required to pay a tax of three percent on the estimated value of the gems. Upon delivery, the person transporting the diamonds would receive one-eighth of the estimated value as a reward. The Company itself reserved the right to buy diamonds from the stock transported for a price at least twenty-five percent higher than the estimated value. After the gentlemen had adopted this plan as a basis for further measures, one of them suddenly produced a letter from Bitter requesting permission to return to Batavia, so that he could petition for a review of the judgment handed down in his divorce suit.[13] Surprised by this unexpected turn of events, the Heren XVII decided to postpone dealing with the matter until a later meeting, when Bitter would be allowed to explain the situation himself. The resolutions passed at subsequent meetings make no reference to the case, however. The Heren XVII had obviously decided to wait and see what the Court of Holland would decide.

As seen above, the Court's decision was not exactly in Bitter's favor, but he had not yet lost the war.[14] It was now clear to him that he would have to return to the East if he wanted to continue his legal battle, and he therefore turned once again to the Heren XVII and asked for "adequate and suitable employ." Bitter's wish was granted. He was reappointed to the Court of Justice, as though nothing had happened. To top it all off, the very next day the diamond trade was formally legalized.[15]

Review—A Legal Last Resort

Judicial review entails the reconsideration and possible reversal of a judgment handed down in court. It has been described as "the ultimate legal remedy, aimed at proving there has been a miscarriage of justice."[16] In Holland cases were rarely submitted to judicial review, but in the Indies the procedure was frequently employed.[17] If one takes a closer look at this legal remedy, one understands immediately why the executive and the judiciary were frequently at loggerheads in the Dutch East Indies. In the seventeenth century the Governor-General and the Council of the Indies often exceeded their powers by meddling in the judicial sphere, there being no clear line of demarcation between the executive and the judiciary.

It sometimes happened that colonial rulers were ordered by their masters in Holland to interfere in judicial matters, and the suit Bitter versus Van Nijenroode is an excellent case in point. We saw how the Heren XVII directed the Governor-General and the Council to repatriate Johan Bitter because of his involvement in diamond smuggling. Then the Court of Justice at Batavia handed down a judgment in a divorce case that was decidedly disadvantageous to the Company employee in question. It is likely that the Councilors arrived at their decision because they felt the Company directors breathing down their necks, though this cannot, of course, be proved. The man in question—himself, ironically enough, a member of the Court of Justice—was denied the opportunity to request a review of the judgment passed at Batavia because the Heren XVII had ordered him to return to Holland immediately. As a conciliatory gesture they advised him to seek redress in Holland. Should we therefore be given to understand that judicial review could only be granted by the States General of the Seven United Provinces, "because the sovereignty in the East Indies over the countries and places, as well as over the inhabitants, whom the Company therefore possesses, derives from the lofty members of the

States General"? Or was it up to the Governor-General and Councilors to admit a case to judicial review? Pieter van Dam, who poses these pertinent questions in his above-mentioned *Beschrijvinge*, gives an immediate answer by explaining that the States General had always advised people who felt they had been treated unfairly by the judicial system in the Indies to return to Batavia and seek redress by lodging an appeal there. A sentence handed down in the Indies could never be subject to judicial review in the Dutch Republic.[18]

The legal historian Van Kan, not entirely satisfied with Van Dam's terse treatment of judicial review, has provided a careful analysis of the historical development of this "judicial emergency brake" in colonial society. Interestingly enough, his account also focuses on the interaction between the executive and judicial branches of government.

According to Van Kan, from the earliest days of the Dutch East India Company people who felt they had been wronged by the judicial system in the Indies had tried to lodge an appeal in Holland, though such appeals were always declared inadmissible. To whom could they then appeal in the Indies? The Court of Justice? No, they were forced to turn to the Governor-General and the Councilors, a custom that Johan Maetsuycker "legalized" when he drew up the Statutes of Batavia.[19] Although the case under review was then brought before the Court of Justice, the admission to the review procedure, which preceded the actual hearing, was decided by the Governor-General and the Councilors. In Van Kan's view, this arrangement regularly resulted in the executive branch actively interfering in the judicial process.[20] Not surprisingly, in 1662 the Heren XVII adopted an amendment that deprived the Governor-General and Councilors of the power to determine which cases would be admitted to judicial review. From that time onward, this power formally resided in the judiciary. In practice, however, the Governor-General and the Councilors continued to "accord review" until the end of the seventeenth century, when the Heren XVII intervened and deprived the High Government of this privilege.

How did judicial review work in Bitter's day? Anyone wishing to contest a judgment could do so within two years of its pronouncement by submitting to the Governor-General and the Councilors a request for a review, which would then be granted or refused. If granted, an ad hoc tribunal was installed, consisting of the Court of Justice augmented by deputy reviewers appointed by the executive. The case was then dealt with by this expanded Court of Justice.

Van Kan describes how Bitter's case was dealt with by the judiciary and the Heren XVII in Holland. He states that the gentlemen had no desire to discuss the wisdom of the judgment passed in Batavia, which is why they told Bitter that the only legal remedy was to request the government of the Indies to admit the case to judicial review in Batavia. According to Van Dam, they did not refer him directly to the Court of Justice, for the simple reason that they preferred to uphold the existing system, and therefore Bitter's case was also referred to the Governor-General and Councilors.

However, we know (unlike Van Dam, who did not have access to all the evidence) that the true story was much more complicated. The Heren XVII were forced to involve the Governor-General and Councilors in this case, because on an earlier occasion the Heren XVII had ordered the government in the Indies to interfere in the legal proceedings in which Bitter was then involved. They had violated their own rules and now felt compelled to put things to rights, causing the legal and administrative organs in Batavia to become inextricably entangled in the matter. Let us return to the ominous autumn of 1683, when Johan Bitter, "sad but ever more accustomed to bearing his own secret sorrows," returned to Batavia.

CHAPTER EIGHT

The So-Called Reconciliation

In the summer of 1679, shortly before Johan Bitter returned to Holland, Nicolaus de Graaff—ship's surgeon, writer, and avid traveler—had returned to Holland from his fifteenth sea voyage. He was fifty-seven years old and thought it high time to say farewell to the wanderer's life. In the hamlet where he settled down, the fishing village

The East Indiaman *Mercurius*, built in 1649. (Pen painting by Willem van de Velde the Elder, Maritiem Museum "Prins Hendrik," Rotterdam)

of Egmond on the Sea, this grizzled adventurer was received with great respect and duly appointed sheriff. De Graaff was quite good at catching scoundrels, but the constant roar of the surf made him yearn for distant shores. Obeying the call of the sea, the elderly globetrotter decided to embark on yet another voyage to the East.

In the spring of 1683 De Graaff entered the service of the Dutch East India Company at Amsterdam and was appointed chief surgeon on the ship *Ridderschap van Holland,* a brand-new East Indiaman. The captain was Jakob Pieterszoon Kool of Zaandam. "We on board the *Ridderschap,*" De Graaff related, "flew the admiral's flag from the topmast, having on board the Honorable Johan Bitter, Councilor of Justice, a wise and modest gentleman who served as admiral of the fleet." The fleet consisted of five ships: *Ridderschap, Cortgene, Coeverden,* and *Castricum* from the Amsterdam Chamber and *Huis te Nek* from Hoorn, which disappeared from view the very first day. It was Commander Bitter's task to keep the ships together for the duration of the voyage, so they could help one another in emergencies. Just how important this was emerges from the fate that befell the above-mentioned *Huis te Nek:* the ship went missing. Another ship, the *Langewijk* of Enkhuizen, whose wayward captain had ordered it to set sail a couple of days earlier, drifted off course to the coast of Angola and did not arrive in Batavia until 8 June 1684, after more than thirteen months at sea.

That spring Bitter had been reappointed to the Court of Justice, "though unwillingly, having preferred a post in the government." Before his departure he said elaborate farewells to his friends in the Amsterdam hostelry. On the morning of 29 April he went to thank the gentlemen of the Amsterdam Chamber for their support and in the afternoon he boarded a yacht that conveyed him to the *Ridderschap,* which he boarded around six o'clock in the evening. The next day Bitter's baggage was inspected and he was required "to hand over four *ams* of wine and a crate of glasses."

Bitter had not counted on this. Not relishing the prospect of a chronically dry throat during the long voyage, he traveled overland the next day to Den Helder to retrieve the confiscated goods. In the meantime the *Ridderschap* was heading across the Zuiderzee toward the island of Texel. After waiting there for a week, the fleet set sail on 9 May. A strong southwesterly wind prevented them from sailing through the Straits of Calais, so they decided to change course for the Shetland Islands, sailing around Scotland and Ireland before heading south.

On 23 June the ships dropped anchor at São Tiago in the Cape Verde islands. The tight-fisted governor of Bitter's first voyage to the East had been replaced by an "honorable, courteous man" who was more than willing to supply the fleet with the necessary provisions.

The stay on São Tiago naturally summoned up sad memories of Johan Bitter's first wife—he must have visited her grave—as well as recollections of his own miraculous recovery. Like an omen, there suddenly appeared on deck a "rough, shaved mendicant monk." Surely this was no coincidence. To Bitter it seemed the right time to thank the Lord, so he took out his purse but, as he recorded in his journal, "Lo and behold! The monk refused to accept the money I offered him, so I kept it."

The fresh provisions were quickly laid in, and the ship could now continue on its way to the equator. This was no easy matter, however, for the fleet was blown far to the east by the south-southwesterly wind. On 8 July Cape Mesurado (in present-day Liberia) was even sighted, though normally the ships should have been on the other side of the ocean by this time, somewhere off the coast of Brazil. Not surprisingly, the ship's council decided to change tack and, with the wind on the port side, to head westward. On 28 July the *Ridderschap*, aided by a gentle breeze, crossed the equator. Neptune came on board with his trident and was given a most gracious welcome by the admiral of the fleet, Johan Bitter. Everyone who was crossing the equator for the first time was subjected to a boisterous initiation rite before being allowed to shake hands with the ruler of the seven seas. One of the "victims" was the commander of the soldiers on board, Dirk Strijker, son of the Dutch consul in Venice. Strijker took it all in stride, but after the simple ritual on deck he resolved to teach the crew how to play-act in earnest. He was certainly qualified to take on this task, for in his youth he had become acquainted in Venice with the *commedia dell'arte* and in Holland he had been one of the driving forces behind the founding of the "renowned theater at Amsterdam."

There was usually a certain amount of tension between the soldiers quartered between-decks and the ship's crew. The soldiers were allowed on deck to get some fresh air only once a day. Weather permitting, they were drilled there, to the accompaniment of bemused comments made by John Company, after which the poor devils disappeared below deck again. Thanks to Strijker, this routine now changed. He took advantage of the beautiful weather and engaged all who were willing in the performance of several comedies. Life on board livened up considerably.

On 5 August the fleet passed Ascension Island, and some time later the Abrolhos Islands, "situated just off the coast of Brazil," were sighted. There, "following an old custom, a thanksgiving feast was held on board the ships; two pigs were slaughtered for the seamen and a fat sheep for the officers." According to their calculations, by the end of August the ships had reached the latitude of the Cape of Good Hope, and the compass course was changed to east. Two weeks later land was sighted and within twenty-four hours the *Ridderschap* dropped anchor in Table Bay, close to the *Cortgene* and the *Castricum*, which had arrived three days earlier. A short while later the *Coeverden* joined the fleet. Commander Bitter was pleased with the safe journey and laid on a banquet, which was also attended by Governor Van der Stel and the most important Company officials stationed at the Cape. "During the toasts," related Nicolaus de Graaff, "many salutes were fired, and three comedies were performed on our ship." Everyone congratulated Dirk Strijker on his troupe of actors, and "after these amusements had made the rounds of all the ships and we had wrapped up business at the Cape, we took our leave and set sail on the last day of September." The rest of the voyage went without mishap. At the end of November 1683 the fleet arrived in the bay of Batavia, "having lost, thank heavens, only five men: two died in their bunks, and three were lost overboard and drowned," wrote De Graaff, much relieved.[1] His duties as ship's surgeon had been fulfilled, and he could now hand over the care of the sick to the local surgeons. At the last moment several worthy passengers died, presumably from gorging on too much fresh fruit after their arrival. One of these last-minute victims was Dirk Strijker, the commander who had delighted them all by transforming the ship's deck into an undulating playhouse.

And what about Bitter? With the coast of Java in sight, he left his becalmed ship at eight o'clock in the morning on 26 November and sailed in a sloop to Batavia, where he arrived—as recorded in his journal—that same evening at half past eight.

> I went silently into the fort and was discovered by Signeur Luchtenburgh in front of Mr. Camphuys's door, where the friends, having that day promoted Mr. Casembroodt to the post of Director of Persia, were still making merry, so much so that it caused me some delay. Nevertheless, the Honorable Mr. Speelman [the Governor-General], who had broken free from the group, was amazed at my coming, as was Mr. Bort, who, through disbelief or curiosity, came upstairs with His Honor and addressed me in astonishment, saying, "What are *you* doing here?" From there I went to see my children, though not without pausing to talk to people in town who were still sitting on their porches or strolling along the canals.

It is not difficult to imagine what happened the day he arrived. An anxious Bitter, unable to wait any longer, probably promised some sailors a substantial reward if they would take him to Batavia as quickly as possible. This undoubtedly entailed a whole day of listening to the singing of the rowers and the rhythmic splashing of the oars, and of course feeling the heat of the tropical sun and then watching it sink into the sea to the west. Bitter, at the helm, stared at the town in the distance, where he saw the lights being lit, one by one, in front of the city gate and atop the walls of the Castle. Setting foot on land and then gaining entrance to the fort itself, he unexpectedly found himself in the midst of a company of merrymakers. The bewilderment on the faces of Bort and Speelman, when they suddenly saw, looming up out of the darkness, the man whom they had dismissed three years before as a "useless employee" must have given Bitter a great deal of satisfaction. Then, in a state of elation, he walked through the balmy tropical evening along the canals, past the porches of the stately homes where Batavia's gentlemen sat smoking their pipes. He tried to take it all in, but he could hardly believe his eyes. He was back, and he would make sure everyone knew it!

Presently Bitter found himself standing at his daughter's front door—his beloved Bartha, whom he had missed so much during his stay in Holland. Shortly after his departure, she had married Constantijn Nobel, Jr. Now the moment had come for his daughter and son-in-law to present him with his grandchildren: Aletta, two and a half, and Constantijn, not yet one. No doubt he would hear soon enough how his headstrong wife had been behaving during his absence.

That same evening Cornelia van Nijenroode was told of Bitter's return by a flustered slave who had bumped into him on the street. She probably didn't sleep well that night, and the next day her anxiety must have mounted even more. The fact that her husband had been reappointed to his former post was bad enough, but the rumor that the Heren XVII had given him permission to request a review of his case made her fear the worst. Her only consolation was that Cornelis Speelman was now the Governor-General and that Balthasar Bort had succeeded him as Director-General. Two good friends of hers held the reins of government, and surely she could look to them for protection. For the time being, though, all remained quiet at the house on Tiger Canal: the coach stayed parked inside the gate, and Cornelia did not show herself.

Contrary to what Cornelia had expected, it was not Bitter who knocked on her door three weeks later: it was the president of the church council, accompanied by an elder. These two gentlemen told Cornelia that her recently returned husband had requested permission to attend a meeting of the church council, and his request had been granted. Bitter had heard that during his absence his wife had been allowed to attend the Lord's Supper "on the condition that she first be reconciled with him." When the members of the church council confirmed this, Bitter asked if they were willing to inquire of his wife if she still meant what she had said, and if so, when she intended to be reconciled with him. After everything that had happened, he wanted to know where he stood. The council was surprised by this sudden request, which was bound to have far-reaching consequences for the separated couple. Determined not to let this case prevent their attending to more urgent matters, the council decided to defer judgment for the time being. After Bitter had left, however, the council sent two delegates to speak to Cornelia.[2]

Two gentlemen subsequently went to the house on Tiger Canal to sound out Cornelia's real feelings for Johan Bitter. Because Christmas Eve was only a couple of days away Cornelia played for time. She told them she had been surprised by the sudden return of her husband and begged for some time to think things over "so that she could calmly attend the Christmas service." The two delegates feared that her evasive answer would not be well received, but they nonetheless pronounced themselves willing to convey it to the other members of the council.[3]

Not unexpectedly, the church council—whose meeting on 20 December was again attended by Bitter—was sure that Cornelia was only stalling for time. The gentlemen demanded an immediate reply, informing Cornelia that from now on she would be dealt with according to civil law and ecclesiastical discipline. This severe answer produced results: two days later the president read aloud to the assembled council the letter he had received from Cornelia.

> In answer to the questions put to me by the church council, I do not recall having said, around three years ago in connection with my attendance at the Lord's Supper, that I was reconciled with Mr. Bitter. If the council wishes to conclude from my statement at the time that I declared myself willing to live with Mr. Bitter, then I must explain that these were not my words, as it was not then nor ever will be my intention to do so.
>
> If, however, the honorable gentlemen on the council still maintain that the above-mentioned word "reconciliation" was used by me, then I must say, for the sake of better understanding and by way of clarification, that I take it to mean that I have reconciled myself to the said Mr. Bitter. Not in the sense that I see him as my husband, but that I love him as my fellow human being and fellow Christian. This means that I have laid aside all past feelings of discord, despite my displeasure at the unjust and slanderous treatment to which he subjected me during the hearing. I would like to get along well with him, as indeed I should with all Christian people, and I wish him well in body and soul.
>
> This does not mean, however, that I intend to waive my right to the separation, which was granted to me after much difficulty in a just manner by the highest court in the land, to whose judgment I shall adhere until it please the Lord God to make my heart and soul feel otherwise. This said, I think I may continue to attend the Lord's Supper with a clear conscience, this being a right that ought not to be contested by the honorable church council.

One thing was clear: Cornelia did not want Johan back under any circumstances. This was her message to the church council and Bitter alike. The elders concluded that she had been pulling the wool over their eyes for three whole years, and they promptly banned Cornelia van Nijenroode from the Lord's Supper, to prevent the pious "from taking part in her sins."[4]

Stubbornly, Bitter asked for and received from the church council copies of all the resolutions concerning him that had been passed in recent weeks, including the letter sent them by Cornelia. He needed these documents to prove to the High Government that judicial review of his case was essential: after all, his wife steadfastly refused to bend. Meanwhile, Cornelia had not been sitting still. Fearing that Bitter would once again manage to lay hold of her property, she succeeded in spiriting away 10,000 rixdollars before it was too late.[5]

Everything now seemed to conspire to bring about Cornelia's ruin. Even her most influential friends could no longer be counted on to help her. Cornelis Speelman's health was declining daily: he suffered from recurring bouts of dropsy and chronic pain as a result of kidney stones, constant reminders of his dissolute younger years. Since the last week of December the Governor-General had no longer appeared in public. When the members of the Council of the Indies, apart from Director-General Bort who was also sick in bed, made their way to Speelman's house to toast his health and wish him a happy new year, the "old lion" was already too weak to receive his cohorts.[6]

Four days later Speelman dictated his last will and testament. The sickly Director-General Balthasar Bort, Jacob van Dam (his secretary), and Andries Cleyer (his personal physician) were named executors of the will, which contained instructions for disposing of his sizable estate. To help these gentlemen sort out "the household affairs, the contents of the linen chests, and so on," Speelman called on the assistance of three of his best lady friends, one of whom was Cornelia van Nijenroode. On 11 January 1684 the Governor-General died "after three days of great distress and unbearable pain from dropsy and other ailments." Two hours later his example was followed by Balthasar Bort, who "after a long and debilitating illness also went the way of all flesh, finding eternal bliss at the age of fifty-eight."[7]

An incredibly opulent funeral followed, costing no less than 13,790 rixdollars. In his *Oud en Nieuw Oost-Indiën*, Valentijn gives a detailed description of this event. As at the funeral of Petronella Wonderaer, Cornelia was on hand to accept condolences, after which, as was the custom, the guests were regaled with food and drink.[8] This was to be Cornelia's last public appearance. After the death of these two men, a new generation of administrators took over, and she no longer had any friends in high places.

Just how fast her influence was waning emerges from the revised judgment handed down by the Court of Justice on 9 May 1684. The separation granted in 1679 was declared null and void. Cornelia was ordered to open up the house on Tiger Canal to her husband and to live with him in peace and the fear of God. The right to manage and dispose of her assets was restored to her husband, as was his right to half her income and the interest accruing from it.[9]

Peace and Harmony

Cornelia van Nijenroode barricaded herself in the house on Tiger Canal and prepared for the worst, but—miracle of miracles—it was a kind and courteous Bitter who appeared at the house a few days later. And, what was even more unbelievable, he seemed to bear no grudge against her.

How she has aged, he must have thought, when he saw her again after all those years. She won't last long. Perhaps he admitted that in the past he had overdone things a bit. Forgive and forget! They were too old to go on squabbling about worldly goods. Now that their accounts were squared, they would do better to put the past behind them and look to the future, for the sake of their own well-being as well as that of their children. One may well imagine that Cornelia's heart stood still upon hearing the word "accounts," though now—sadder but wiser—she may have been able to restrain herself.

To everyone's surprise, their own included, the couple managed to work out a *modus vivendi*, or so it seemed. Every Sunday their extended family attended church together: the procession was headed by several slaves who cleared the way, followed by Bitter with his wife on his arm, the children from their previous marriages, and in their wake a male slave carrying Cornelia's prie-dieu chair and a female slave bearing the splendid betel box that her first husband, Pieter Cnoll, had given her. In short, they presented the very picture of harmony.

At the end of September, only three months after the beginning of their "second marriage," the couple humbly requested to be allowed to attend the Lord's Supper.[10] Full of lofty feelings inspired by this miraculous about-face, the church council welcomed the lost sheep back to the fold. Cornelia, that is, was welcomed back immediately, but Bitter was told that, although his presence at the Lord's table would also be greatly appreciated, there were some problems that had to be resolved first.

One glance at the scowl on Reverend Zas's face and Bitter knew what they were referring to. He assumed a contrite expression and said that he would gladly apologize for his rude behavior of seven years ago. And if Reverend Zas would be so kind as to accept his heartfelt apology, then he would be a happy—even grateful—man. Again the pious gentlemen must have breathed a collective sigh of relief and thanked the Good Shepherd for Bitter's contrition. And just as the Lord God forgives transgressors, the church councilors also forgave these two sorry sinners.[11] To make the happy ending complete, Bitter's youngest daughters, who were still boarding with the Couper family, were again welcomed into the house on Tiger Canal.[12] Cornelia's son, Cornelis Cnoll, together with his wife and children, had already taken up residence next door. The only note of discord in this "close harmony" was sounded by Bitter, when it was discovered that he had again dipped into his wife's assets to pay off some old debts. Cornelia did not seem to mind, however. She agreed that her husband needed some freedom of movement, and she was now willing to give it to him in exchange for domestic tranquility. Peace had been restored to their household, and they managed to live together in harmony, or, as Bitter later put it, in "reasonable concord, except for an occasional fit of temper on her part."[13]

It all seemed too good to be true, and indeed it was. The couple might have managed to live together in harmony if the children had not spoiled it all. Children, especially daughters-in-law, tend to speak their mind, saying things out loud that parents would sooner leave unspoken. This frankness soon proved to be the couple's undoing. In August 1685, after a year and a half of relative quiet, all hell broke loose.

Several days earlier, Bitter—pursuing his policy of peaceful Cnoll-existence—had finally achieved his objective. After finding out how much money Cornelia had deposited with the Company, he had 20,000 rixdollars, which up to then had been kept in the name of the deceased Pieter Cnoll, transferred to his own account. Bitter's attempts to explain away his actions—this move would supposedly enable him to manage the money more effectively—were greeted with incredulity. It began to dawn upon the family that Bitter had only been playing for time in order to achieve, an inch at a time, his original goal. The first person to bring the subject out into the open was his daughter-in-law, Hillegonda Dubbeldecop, the wife of Cornelis Cnoll.

The Resumption of Hostilities

On the afternoon of 25 August, Cornelia, two lady friends, and her daughter-in-law were having a cup of tea when Bitter entered the room. We do not know whether he again held a mirror up to his wife's face, but his behavior was such that Hillegonda became furious and called him a "beast." This elicited a retort of "scandalmonger," and before anyone knew what was happening, the two began hitting each other, while Cornelia shrieked, "My daughter, my child." Within seconds the room turned into a field of battle. In the words later used by Bitter's lawyer to describe the scene, both mother and daughter-in-law "grabbed the plaintiff by the hair and submitted him to a fierce beating, before he eventually succeeded in pushing away the two malicious wenches."[14] And this was not the only clash. Hostilities soon escalated; forgetting all his good intentions, Bitter now brought in the artillery.

It was already growing dark on the evening of 5 January 1686 when three sailmakers happened to be returning from town to the pier. Walking down Tiger Canal they were treated to a curious sight: a middle-aged gentleman chasing an elderly lady down the street. When they saw him grab her by the hair and drag her to the entrance of a large house, the men intervened. While they were inspecting the poor woman's wounds—she was bleeding from the mouth—the assailant fled. A notary was quickly called to the scene to record the details of this nasty incident. The sailmakers testified under oath to what they had seen and heard: "You whore, you beast, you bitch, come here and I'll trample you underfoot until the blood gushes from your mouth."[15]

These words had scarcely been noted down when the culprit himself reappeared, this time with the sheriff and his helpers in tow. Bitter introduced himself as a member of the Court of Justice, and when he heard that they had made a sworn statement, he shouted, "You bought dogs, tell me how much she paid you," adding, "What is my wife to you? What does it matter to you if I scold my wife all day long?" Receiving no reply, Bitter then gestured toward the sailmakers and ordered the sheriff to arrest them. Handcuffed like criminals, the three witnesses were escorted to the office of the provost sergeant, where Bitter subjected them to a cross-examination.[16] Realizing he was getting nowhere, he suddenly switched tactics. "Come on, lads," he said ingratiatingly, "change your testimony and I'll let you go unharmed." When this approach met with a flat refusal, the interrogator continued, "Upon my word, I'll make you pay for this." And pay they did. The three sail-makers were locked up and clapped into irons.[17] One night of trying to sleep between the cockroaches and the mildewed walls was enough to make the three cavaliers change their mind. They retracted their statement and signed another one, declaring the first to be null and void, in return for which they were released. Bitter, ever attentive to details, gave them each a quarter to ease their hunger.

Bitter's colleagues, who later got wind of what had really happened, were unable to condone such high-handed behavior: he had really overstepped the bounds of his authority this time. No immediate disci-plinary action was taken, however. Perhaps they still found Bitter to be a hard worker who took his job seriously, quite a decent fellow, actual-ly, as long as one kept quiet about his marital woes.

Cornelia soon found herself in a position to hear what the authori-ties thought of it all. She discovered that, without her knowledge, her husband had sent more bills of exchange to his friends in Holland, this time to the tune of 12,765 rixdollars. The ships had already sailed, so there was nothing she could do but write it off as a loss. In order to safe-guard the 8,000 rixdollars still deposited with the Company in Cnoll's name, she wrote to the Governor-General and Councilors, telling them that Bitter was planning to transfer this sum to an account belonging to a man named Frans Gade. Her request that the money not be touched was granted.[18]

The Precedent

Let us interrupt these latest skirmishes to take a look at the history of the case up to this point. The drama starring Cornelia van Nijenroode represents one of the rare instances in which a second lawsuit presented itself with the same charge as the first, while the cast of characters—the leading players, the church council, the Court of Justice, and the Council of the Indies—likewise remained the same. Perhaps I should say more or less the same, because both the institutions and the persons involved had changed somewhat over the years, though the battlefield and the stakes had not. What had changed were the external factors influencing the decision-making process. Played out against this shifting backdrop is the story of a man who steals his wife's possessions and beats her for good measure; then, after being reprimanded, he does the same thing all over again.

We must now delve into the matter more deeply: women at that time did not have the legal right to manage their own assets, but did society in fact offer Cornelia a way of getting around the law? When lawyers speak of a precedent, they cite a case, heard under comparable circumstances in the past, whose example may help them to solve a complex legal problem. Legal precedence was Cornelia's biggest problem. The court of law—actually her last resort—had at first refused to grant her the separation she had asked for. What help could she now expect in her legal battle against her husband from a court that had in fact ruled that her property was not really her own? She was fighting a losing battle. The legal incapacity of women to manage their own affairs meant that Cornelia could expect no more help from legal quarters. It is important to realize this, otherwise one could easily get the impression—from subsequent events, as well as from the way in which Cornelia formulated her protests—that it was only the partiality of the Court of Justice that stood in the way of resolving the conflict.

But things were not so simple. We are not dealing here with a proto-feminist. Under the circumstances it was simply not possible for Cornelia to denounce the unfair treatment to which women were legally subjected. She did hope, however, that as an old, spent woman she would ultimately triumph, if only she persevered and succeeded in demonstrating the patent unfairness of her adversary's claims. We will now take a closer look at her tactics and see whether she was right in assuming that sympathy and understanding would ensure her ultimate triumph.

A Question of Politics

Earlier on we saw how the Governor-General and the Councilors of the Indies intervened directly to freeze the 8,000 rixdollars belonging to Cornelia that were still deposited with the Company. Encouraged by this stopgap measure taken by the authorities and buoyed up by the thought that she had not been abandoned entirely, Cornelia now revealed her innermost feelings in a second letter to the High Government. She begged for the right to live apart from her husband, so that he could no longer mistreat her. She also requested safeguards that would prevent him from gaining access to her goods and slaves while her request was pending. Her request, however, was denied. The Council of the Indies considered the matter outside its competence and, unfortunately for Cornelia, forwarded her request to the Court of Justice.

If we look at the minutes of the meeting of 1 May 1686, when this resolution was passed, our attention is drawn to a short note written in the margin by Governor-General Johannes Camphuys. He was, theoretically, in agreement with the decision but remarked that under certain circumstances the government should not shy away from taking the "political" steps necessary to maintain law and order and to preserve the peace.[19] In other words, the High Government, for reasons of its own, should feel free to intervene if such intervention meant that justice would ultimately be served. His remarks would not have reached Cornelia in exactly these words, but it is likely that she got wind of the gist of it. It is possible that the contents of her first letter, of which no copy has been preserved, elicited these remarks from Camphuys. In any case, a second request submitted by Cornelia has been preserved in full. In this letter she picks up the lifeline thrown to her by the Governor-General and does not hesitate to expand on his ideas.

Cornelia begins by expressing her regret at the fact that the Governor-General and Councilors forwarded her request to the Court of Justice. Considering her moderate tone and the reasonableness of her demands, she thought "it would not have been difficult for Your Lordships to take political measures aimed at preventing mischief and further troubles." She then argued that she was no longer asking for a legal separation, because this would result in stipulations requiring each of the partners to live by his or her own means, and Bitter would never consent to that. Instead she was asking only for protective measures to safeguard both her personal security and her fortune. If the Council of the Indies had granted this request, no one would have felt that legal steps had been taken or that the Council had usurped the rights of the Court of Justice. Administrative intervention of this kind would have restored law and order.

Now that she had revealed her thoughts and course of action to the Council of the Indies, Cornelia ventured to explain why she preferred not to appeal to the Court of Justice in this matter. It had never been her intention to reveal her motives, but now that the authorities had referred her case to the Court, she felt there were certain points that needed elucidation. Actually, it all boiled down to the fact that she had no faith in Bitter's colleagues. Nevertheless, the supplicant again beseeched the High Government to take political action, either by means of mediation or by issuing an outright order. If the authorities denied her request, she wished to clarify her doubts as to the integrity of the Court of Justice.[20]

The Council of the Indies was in a quandary; Cornelia's request did not seem unreasonable. We already know Governor-General Camphuys's opinion. Willem van Outhoorn, a Councilor of the Indies who also presided over the Court of Justice, asked to be excused from taking

part in the proceedings. The decision that was finally taken was equiv-
ocal. The High Government was of the opinion that the couple should
try once again to work out a separation agreeable to both of them. Two
members of the Council of the Indies, Director-General Anthony
Hurdt and Gerard de Bevere, were asked to mediate in the dispute. In
fact, this decision was contrary to everything Bitter had been fighting
for in his attempt to gain total control over Cornelia's fortune.

Little headway was made for several months. The next mention of
the case refers to a request made by Johan Bitter, which was discussed
by the Governor-General and the Councilors at a meeting held on 20
August 1686. Bitter introduced himself as the husband who "has been
so much pushed about and pestered by his wife since his wedding day
that the whole town pities him." He recounted how things had gone
since his return to Batavia. In the beginning he was forced to live in a
miserable shack, and it was only later that he was allowed to move back
into his house, thanks to the revised judgment of the Batavian court.
Unfortunately, his wife continued to make life difficult for him, "constantly rearing her ugly head, vilifying her husband and giving his children a drubbing till they were driven out of the house, yea, even dragging his name through the mud as though he were a man of troublesome, not to say evil, ways." As a man of honor, he requested the
authorities to send two gentlemen to warn his wife to stop spouting
such slanderous lies, as this was to the detriment of his position on the
Court of Justice.[21]

A recent incident had given Bitter cause to write this letter: once
again the couple had treated Batavian society to a distasteful spectacle.
Near the end of July one of their nocturnal quarrels had degenerated
into a street brawl. Around midnight several witnesses saw Bitter dragging his wife by her hair down the street and heard her screaming,
"Help! Murder!" Worried about the malicious gossip his barbarous
behavior might provoke, that same night Bitter knocked on the door
of his neighbor, Reverend Vosmaer. When the door was opened, he

whined, "See what a shrew I married! She threw a handful of sand in my face! Just look at me!" Vosmaer's wife, who was sick and tired of all her neighbors' bickering, retorted, "I'll have nothing to do with you or the quarrels between you and your wife."[22] Although Bitter muttered something about her complete lack of sympathy, he did not realize—as we are able to with the wisdom of hindsight—that this incident was one of the first signs that the whole community was getting fed up with the Bitters' marital squabbles.

We should not, however, jump to the conclusion, after hearing the remarks made by Reverend Vosmaer's wife, that the church now intended to retreat from the field of battle. It is surprising, nonetheless, that starting in the spring of 1686 the minutes of the council's meetings no longer contain any references to the couple. The church council seemed to have given up all hope of their ever becoming reconciled. The above-mentioned incident—as well as the news that Bitter had a soldier billeted in the house to keep an eye on his wife, not to mention the accusation that he was sleeping with Lucretia, one of her house slaves—must surely have diminished the esteem in which the Governor-General and Council still seemed to hold the Councilor of Justice.

On 25 November 1686 Director-General Anthony Hurdt and Gerard de Bevere filed their report on their attempts at mediation. They confirmed what their colleagues had already predicted: their mission had been a complete failure. The Councilors were granted extra time to ask themselves if there was any point in taking further measures. Five days later they announced their decision: Cornelia's request "to be allowed to live separately . . . as a political measure" was denied, though she was given the chance to appear before the Governor-General and the Council of the Indies to voice the objections she had raised against the Court of Justice. Unfortunately, there is no record of what these objections actually were, but she probably complained that her husband's associates were in league with him.

Cornelia certainly felt abandoned. By the end of 1686 she was even denied access to her own home. "Papa Bitter has forbidden you to enter," her own slaves said to her in Portuguese from behind closed doors.[23] To be denied entrance by one's own slaves—it was impossible to sink any lower in Batavian society. By this time the conflict had risen to such a pitch that Governor-General Camphuys was no longer interested in who the guilty party was. His conclusion reads as follows: "Without actually knowing who caused the argument, we agree with the old adage 'it takes two to make a quarrel.'"[24]

Neither the Christmas spirit nor their New Year's resolutions caused either party to repent. Bitter even spent the holidays making a list of all his grievances. Notary Van Es's first official business of the new year was to record word for word Bitter's litany of complaints about his wife: she had been unfaithful to him since their wedding day, she was full of "evil, spite, sinister incorrigibility, cunning, and falsehood." To this declaration was added an affidavit from the notary himself, testifying that he had entered Cornelia's bedchamber one night and ordered her to lie with her husband as a good wife should and that his order had been met with a flat refusal. Both documents were handed over to the Court. When Cornelia was informed of their contents she immediately demanded that her husband prove his allegations. Now it was Bitter's turn: he complained to the Governor-General and the Councilors that his wife was constantly smuggling valuable objects out of the house, which is why he was asking permission to institute legal proceedings against her. He also asked for copies of all the letters his wife had recently written to the authorities.

This was the last straw. The Council of the Indies decided on 15 January 1687 to put an end to all this trouble and passed an extraordinary resolution: Master of Laws Johan Bitter and his lawfully wedded wife Cornelia van Nijenroode were both served notice—separately, of course—that in the event of their failing to reach a swift settlement, they would have to return to Holland with the homeward-bound fleet in the autumn.[25] The case had become such a threat to law and order and such a waste of time for the authorities who had to deal with it that the only solution was to ship the quarreling couple off to Holland. The legal doctors, having found no medicine to cure the malignancy, had finally opted for surgical removal of the cantankerous tumor.

CHAPTER NINE

The Last Round

In his General Missive of 1687 to the Heren XVII, Governor-General Camphuys devoted no fewer than eleven pages to the latest developments surrounding the affair that was the talk of the town. He referred anyone desiring further details to the twenty-two resolutions passed by himself and the Council of the Indies between 15 January 1687 and 15 December 1687, the day on which Cornelia departed for Holland. In any event, the High Government had washed its hands of the matter and ordered the recalcitrant couple to sail on the next homeward-bound fleet.

> The two of them will have to decide on any further steps to be taken; we will no longer deal with this tedious matter, which in the light of our many duties has been nothing but a daily source of fatigue. We respectfully refer to the resolutions already passed.

Camphuys had every reason to complain. The case had been preying on his mind for the past twelve months, even though this was partly his own fault. After the High Government had decided a year earlier to deny Bitter and his wife further access to the Court of Justice and had advised them to "air their differences before a court in the fatherland," it had soon dawned on him that if there is no judge, people will be their own judge and jury. The Governor-General had therefore been forced to take measures to safeguard Cornelia's position. Johan Bitter had admittedly been denied recourse to the law as far as the divorce case was concerned, but in other matters he was still allowed to institute proceedings. It is hardly surprising, therefore, that until the day of embarkation he continued to pursue his course of deliberate provocation and to conduct his relentless search for legal loopholes.

Throughout the year Cornelia van Nijenroode continued to demonstrate her characteristic perseverance, though her health eventually showed signs of worsening. She increasingly came to depend for support on her only surviving child, 29-year-old Cornelis. Until now I have mentioned young Cnoll only in passing—when he treated the slave Untung so badly that he fled, for example, and when his bold wife Hillegonda dared to defy Bitter—but now it is time to devote some attention to him.

After all his siblings had died, Cornelis Cnoll became heir to the entire 40,000 rixdollars that Pieter Cnoll had left to his children. Upon coming of age—twenty-four in those days—Cornelis had become a wealthy man overnight. He therefore requested an honorable discharge from the rank of army sergeant, as he wanted to spend the rest of his life as a freeburgher of independent means.[1] On 7 June 1678 he was elected to the honorary post of ensign of the civic guards, and on 30 August, when the guards marched as usual to the large square to parade before the Governor-General and the assembled company, Cornelia, the proud mother, also stood in the flower-festooned marquee, enjoying the spectacle amid the Councilors of the Indies and their wives and other high-ranking members of society. After the various companies had lined up in front of the marquee, she witnessed her son being installed "in front of his people, with courage and the utmost decorum." Like father, like son, she must have thought. The good old days seemed to have returned.[2]

Cornelis Cnoll had another important reason for putting life in the barracks behind him: he was planning to marry the above-mentioned

Hillegonda Dubbeldecop. Apart from the argument between Cornelis and his stepfather concerning the use of his horse, there was no mention of an open conflict between the two until 1686, by which time Cornelis occupied a seat on the recently formed polder board.

Cornelis lived in a house bordering on his parents' back garden, making it easy for him and his wife to visit his mother. But when these visits began to get on Johan Bitter's nerves, he had an iron fence built around his house to keep his stepson out. Cornelis would not accept defeat, however, and pulled down the fence with his own hands, no doubt with his mother's approval. At Bitter's request, Cornelis was summoned to appear before the Bench of Aldermen and fined 125 guilders for misconduct.[3] Cornelis was no longer prepared to play the role of little boy. He was a man now, ready and willing to bend iron railings for his mother if necessary. Cornelia, happy to have her son at her side, secretly transferred some of her money to his account. This did not go unnoticed. Her jealous husband immediately took legal action and had his stepson brought before the Bench of Aldermen to force him to reveal how much money his mother had given him.

When Cornelia made her objections known in a long letter dated 18 March 1687 to the Governor-General and the Council of the Indies, she sent her son as her spokesman to inform the authorities that she would comply with their decision.

> Having heard that Your Lordships have decided that she and her husband Johan Bitter must depart for Holland, she complies with the order, though regretfully, dreading such a long voyage owing to her old age and weak constitution.... It is only the fear of having to endure blows, scorn, humiliation, and other indignities that enables her to accept such a cruel fate.... And being forced to choose the easier path, she intends to go to the fatherland and await the decision of the court there.

While awaiting her departure, however, she begged the authorities to oblige her by granting a whole list of requests, which included the following:

- that she be allowed to live apart from her husband in Batavia, to avoid being mistreated by him;
- that she be allowed to sail on a different ship to prevent further calamity;
- that until the day of embarkation she be allowed to keep as many slaves as she needed (of the thirty who remained) to wait on her (at the time of her petition she had one male and four female slaves, whereas Bitter had sixteen male and nine female slaves at his disposal);
- that it be decided who should live in the house, or whether it should be sold immediately;
- that she be allowed to go to the house to fetch the clothing her husband had hidden, "forcing the supplicant to go to church wearing a black sarong";
- that an inventory be made of all her personal effects;
- that the entire proceeds of the sale of the house, the furniture, and the slaves be paid into her account;
- that the Orphans' Chamber assume the administration of the 8,000 rixdollars belonging to her, but leave them on deposit with the Company; likewise the 12,765 rixdollars that her husband still claimed to have in his possession;
- that her husband be denied the right to enter into contracts using the money in her account;
- that she be paid a daily allowance from the goods seized by the sequestrator;
- that declarations made at an earlier stage in the proceedings be reaffirmed in writing for later reference.[4]

As mentioned above, Cornelis took it upon himself to inform the Council of the Indies of the contents of this letter. Not much went unnoticed in Batavia. Three days later, on 21 March, Bitter filed a petition voicing his suspicions that his stepson had again taken action against him "on behalf of that troublesome mother of his." He therefore requested a written statement of all that had been discussed at the meeting, for "not only the law of nature but also that of all peoples teaches us that each party should know the other's standpoint."[5]

This request was denied. Desperate, Bitter now reached one last time into his bag of tricks and accused his wife of practicing black magic. On 26 March Bitter summoned five "Moorish priests" to his house and showed them a jug covered with a strange black substance. This *corpus delicti* had been hidden in his home, he informed them. It truly seemed as though someone wanted to hurt the master of the house. The "sorcerers" were asked to examine the object closely, and the notary Van Es was on hand to record their findings. First the black substance was removed; then the underside of the jug was inspected. Affixed to it was a square piece of paper covered in Arabic letters. Inside the jug, on the bottom, the exorcists found a little doll with devilish features. Their conclusion was unequivocal: this jug had been put there by someone bent on doing evil, and its purpose was to induce a protracted illness. The priests, however, admitted that the writing yielded no clues as to the identity of the intended victim, the person who had ordered the black magic, or the author of the letter. Nor could they say who the ugly little doll was supposed to represent. Black magic was a common occurrence in Batavia, but it seemed far-fetched to accuse Cornelia of sorcery. At any rate, the accusations were not taken seriously.

When this witch-hunt proved futile Bitter once again targeted Cornelia's son. Cornelis Cnoll had at first been acquitted by the Bench of Aldermen of the charge that he and Cornelia had spirited away money, but Bitter had lodged an appeal and this time the judgment was in his favor. The court now ordered Cornelis Cnoll to disclose which of his mother's assets had recently come into his possession. He refused to comply with the order, appealing instead on 15 April to the Council of the Indies for permission to request a review of the judgment. His request was granted, though Bitter took no notice of it and continued with all the means at his disposal to pressure his stepson to declare under oath "which assets he had had in his possession at the time of his arrest."[6] Cornelis thereupon approached the Governor-General and Councilors and asked them to call a halt to Bitter's action until his case had been reviewed.

This was a shrewd move, for Cornelis Cnoll intended to use the full two years allotted for the preparation of a case. He also said that he wanted to send all the documents to legal scholars in Holland, "as is the custom here in the Indies, for without their advice one cannot have much hope of triumphing, since those appointed to reconsider the case are seldom trained lawyers."

The High Government stayed the proceedings and decided to ask the opinion of the Governor-General, who had been absent when the request was read. A month later they still had not made up their minds. Furious at such procrastination, Bitter demanded on 22 July that Cornelis's request for a review be declared "sly and underhand." The date of his departure was approaching and a postponement was not to his advantage.[7] A week later the Council of the Indies decided to give Cornelis Cnoll the full two years he had asked for, which meant that Bitter had just missed his last chance of laying his hands on Cornelia's fortune in Batavia.

Cornelia was not making any headway either. When she realized that the Council of the Indies was not going to answer her letter, she complained again on 15 August that her suspicions had not been without foundation: slowly but surely, Bitter was making off with the last of her assets. She called for immediate action. To emphasize her plight she enclosed a sworn statement from the notary Frederik Michault, who two days previously had attempted, at her request, to gain entry to her bedchamber to fetch the personal papers she kept there. This room had been sealed since she had fled her home.

Michault had been summoned by his colleague Van Es to appear at Bitter's house at three o'clock in the afternoon, but he was kept waiting several hours before being told he could break the seal. When at last he prepared to do so, he discovered that the seal had already been broken. Bitter feigned astonishment but then flew into a rage when his deception became obvious. Michault was eventually thrown out of the house amid great tumult.[8]

Seven days later the still furious Bitter appeared before the Council of the Indies and loudly demanded "that his wife, with all her base tricks and wily ways aimed at vilifying her lawfully wedded husband and guardian, should no longer be given a hearing until she had fulfilled her obligation to disclose the full extent of the assets in her possession on their wedding day." Only when she had complied with this order would he agree to have his books audited.[9]

The Authorities Lose Patience

The Governor-General and the Councilors considered both requests, saw that all hopes of reconciliation had been in vain, and decided it was now time to cut the Gordian knot: two supervisory guardians were appointed to administer, until the day of Bitter's embarkation, the property formerly belonging to Pieter Cnoll. The supervisory guardians were also ordered to sell all of Cornelia's possessions. The proceeds of the sale, as well as the money that had been sequestered, would be entrusted to the judge in Holland, who would see to it that the money was given to the rightful owner after final judgment was passed.[10]

One member of the Council of the Indies, Gerard de Bevere, a lawyer by profession, did not agree with this extraordinary decision and expressed a different opinion in his own advisory report. He wrote that he could not understand why Bitter was being deprived of his conjugal rights "under a specious pretext, as though he had squandered her

money, which she has never been able to prove." In De Bevere's opinion, the revised judgment of 9 May 1684 gave Bitter the right to half
the income and interest accruing from his wife's assets, as well as the
right to manage and dispose of her property as he saw fit. After all, even
before the separation had been granted, Cornelia had been ordered to
disclose to her husband the true extent of her fortune from their wedding day onward. According to De Bevere, Cornelia had never complied with this order, although she was bound by law to do so: "[Bitter
possesses] by law the authority to rule over his wife as her husband and
guardian, a fact that was roundly affirmed in the court's ruling." De
Bevere therefore concluded that the Governor-General and Councilors should deny Cornelia's request to be placed under the protection of
supervisory guardians, which was "an outrageous demand and much to
the detriment of her husband."[11]

Although De Bevere was right, legally speaking, his colleagues
would not accept his arguments. They stuck to their decision; all of
them, that is, except the president of the Court of Justice, Willem van
Outhoorn. He refused to elaborate on his reasons for not concurring
with their decision; he simply refused to have anything to do with the
case. Van Outhoorn had been born in the Moluccas and was truly a
man of the Indies, having spent only a short time in the Dutch
Republic to finish off his studies at the University of Leiden. He had
loathed the quarrelsome Bitter ever since he and Cornelis Speelman
had acted as witnesses to Bitter's dealings with Van Becom in 1679, and
his antipathy had if anything increased during the many sessions of the
Court of Justice he had since presided over. Van Outhoorn reiterated
his refusal to take part in the proceedings.[12]

On 29 August Johan Bitter was summoned to appear before the
Governor-General, who informed him of the Council's decision. As
was only to be expected, Bitter objected to the idea of appointing
supervisory guardians, but because his wife was willing to comply with
the decision—indeed, she was the one who had requested it—the

Councilors Willem ten Rhijne and Daniel van der Bolk were appointed to seize Cornelia's possessions, as well as the disputed capital that Johan Bitter had deposited with the Company.[13] As a result of these new developments, Cornelis Cnoll felt compelled to ask permission for himself and his family to accompany his mother to Holland in order to lend her support during the hearing there.[14]

Rearguard Action

Johan Bitter had only a few months left to get his affairs in order before departing with the homeward-bound fleet in December. Because he had nothing to lose, he now began to lash out in all directions. First of all, he raked up his old quarrel with Van Becom, not so much to annoy Van Becom as to humiliate the members of the Council of the Indies.

A street scene in Batavia. In the left background a Chinese *wayang* is being performed. (Anonymous, Printroom, Rijksmuseum, Amsterdam)

As we know, years earlier Cornelia van Nijenroode had transferred 3,000 rixdollars to the account of the well-to-do freeburgher Adriaen van Becom, who had stated that it was not his money but the money of "Mistress Cnoll." When Bitter discovered this, he had a summons served on Van Becom, who was ordered to pay the 3,000 rixdollars to Bitter and an additional fine of 50 rixdollars. To mollify the furious Van Becom, Van Outhoorn and Speelman had then required Bitter to sign a letter of remission, an "act of indemnity or non-execution," which seemed to put an end to the matter.

Nearly a decade after the fact, this appeared to have been wishful thinking; Bitter now opened up the wound. He maintained that "he had been threatened by the late Mr. Speelman and forced, to his great detriment," to waive the right to collect his money. The fact that Speelman—the bully in Bitter's version of the story—had meanwhile died did not deter him in the slightest; on the contrary, it suited him just fine.

On 29 August 1687 Johan Bitter filed a petition with the High Government demanding payment from the estate of the late Cornelis Speelman of the 3,000 rixdollars he had been cheated of. This capricious demand was only possible because it was taking so long to wind up Speelman's estate. Three years after his death there was still no end in sight. The former Governor-General had been guilty of a number of shady deals, and the executors of his will were still being besieged by people claiming that Speelman owed them money. To complicate matters, there were still large amounts to be collected from outstanding loans.

In Bitter's case, however, the facts were not in doubt. Except for Speelman, all the persons involved were still living. The current president of the Court of Justice, Willem van Outhoorn, had even been involved directly in the affair, though he did not like to be reminded of it, which was all the more reason for Johan Bitter to rub salt into the wound.

On 9 September 1687 the executors of Speelman's will, Marten Pit and Nicolaas Schagen, presented a memorandum to the Governor-General in which they expressed their surprise at Bitter's seeking redress eight years after the fact, as he should have done so within four. As a lawyer he should have known that such action is permitted only if the claimant can substantiate his charge with hard evidence. Furthermore, they could not understand why a person who had willingly signed a contract in a well-governed town had not complained immediately if he felt he had been wronged.[15] They added that if Bitter were allowed to seek redress, Van Becom would surely lodge an appeal.

The concluding remarks of the executors of Speelman's will are crystal clear: they wished to submit a refutation of Bitter's claim, so that "the calumnies with which Mr. Bitter has so boldly and insolently sullied the memory of such an illustrious person as the Governor-General of the Indies, right under the eyes of Your Lordships of the High Government, shall be expurgated. Otherwise it is to be feared that the said Mr. Bitter (in accordance with the knowledge that they, the executors, have of his temper and character) will seize the opportunity of spreading such unfounded and unopposed lies—both in the fatherland and elsewhere—imputing the use of threats and force to a deceased man who can no longer defend himself."[16]

After a bit of internal squabbling, the Council of the Indies proved implacable. On the condition that he come up with some hard proof to substantiate his claims against Speelman, Bitter was granted the right to seek redress, even though the deadline for lodging an appeal had elapsed. It appeared, however, that he was unable to come up with any fresh evidence. By now Bitter was beginning to get on everyone's nerves, and this had obviously been his intention all along.

The administrative elite had hit back hard, and now it was the turn of Bitter's colleagues on the Court of Justice to turn against him. If Bitter was bent on being a nuisance, they were determined to find a skeleton in his closet, too. The public prosecutor, Gualtherus Zeeman, summoned Johan Bitter to appear in court for the arrest and unlawful detention of the three sailmakers who had intervened in the couple's street brawl the year before. Two of the sailmakers were still in Batavia; the third had meanwhile left for Ternate. This was reason enough for the Court to pronounce an interlocutory judgment, giving the prosecutor the green light to institute proceedings against Bitter. Bitter in turn attempted to have this interlocutory order overturned, requesting that all witnesses be summoned first. When his request was denied on 18 November, Bitter raised objections to the participation of one of the members of the Council of the Indies, Willem ten Rhijne. Bitter maintained that Ten Rhijne, who was also a member of the Court of Justice, should not take part in the public prosecutor's case against him because he was a drunkard, adding that Ten Rhijne's colleague Nicolaas Schagen had told him so in confidence. Governor-General Camphuys, whose relations with the Council of the Indies were rather strained, said that in his dealings with the Council it had not escaped his notice that Ten Rhijne really did have a drinking problem. Upon hearing this remark Schagen could do nothing but make a lame excuse, mumbling that "the allegations of constant drunkenness of the said Ten Rhijne were nothing more than a manner of speaking, meaning that he likes his liquor, that he often reaches for the bottle at unseemly times, in public and in full view of everyone, and is mocked by the whole world, as everyone in Batavia knows perfectly well!"[17] Bitter eventually got off with a reprimand, but in the meantime he had succeeded in making the Court of Justice and the High Government look like a bunch of fools.

While Johan Bitter continued to stir up trouble wherever he could, preparations were under way for the voyage of the homeward-bound fleet. In September the first five ships were chosen: *'s Landts Welvaren*, *Waalstroom*, *Zallant*, *Sion*, and *Goudestein*. On 31 October they were declared seaworthy: "of good, sound wood, watertight and well-made, without the slightest defect."[18] It was not proving easy, however, to find enough crew members. The tropical climate and the regular outbreak of epidemics in Batavia claimed many lives among the sailors. On 18 November Cornelis Cnoll's request to take along a cook and a "black wet nurse for his infant child" was granted. A few days later his mother was also given permission to take along a maidservant "to attend her and help her, owing to her weak condition." Bitter was allowed to take two slaves as far as Cape Town.[19]

The two sequestrators, Daniel van der Bolk and Willem ten Rhijne (the very man Bitter had accused of drunkenness), now thought it time to go into action. They had been appointed by the High Government to sell all the worldly goods belonging to Johan Bitter and Cornelia van Nijenroode. At first Bitter had also protested against the appointment of Van der Bolk "because he was younger in years" than Bitter, but this ridiculous objection had been dismissed. The public sale of Cornelia's possessions began on 2 December, and within a few days everything had been sold: the household effects, the coach, the horses, and the slaves. Ten Rhijne and Van der Bolk were astonished to learn that a few days earlier Bitter had secretly sold the house to his henchman Jacob Does for the ridiculously low price of 6,500 rixdollars.

This sale had taken place despite previous agreements between Bitter and his stepson, Cornelis, who had intended to buy the house from his mother and stepfather. When Cnoll demanded to know why he had sold the house to Does, Bitter replied that he saw no reason not to. After all, his stepson had let it be known that he intended to accompany his mother to Holland, and in his view this released him from any obligation whatever.

Cnoll's protests were in vain; he was told by the authorities that he would have to discuss the matter with Does himself. When he attempted to do so, Does retorted that Cornelia still owed him 1,000 rixdollars.[20] Moreover, he did not wish to discuss the purchase agreement with a third party (Cornelis Cnoll); he had bought the house from Bitter and did not intend to sell it. Cornelis talked till he was blue in the face; Does was not to be moved. When he had declared himself willing to accompany his mother to Holland to lend her support during the hearing, he had neglected to say that he eventually wanted to return to Batavia, the place of his birth. Both mother and son were so resentful that they refused to pay Does the money they owed him. At the latter's request the sequestrators deducted this amount from the proceeds of the sale, and so Does finally received his 1,000 rixdollars after all.[21]

During the autumn of 1687 Cornelia and Johan undoubtedly clashed again, but nothing could prevent the inevitable. On 16 January 1688 the hour had come. Johan Bitter, "after finally winding up his affairs," departed with a large entourage from the sloops' landing stage "in a swift vessel" in the company of his two youngest daughters. Bartha stayed behind with her family; his son Arnolt had already been sent to the Netherlands. Taking leave of his favorite daughter Bartha must have been especially difficult for Bitter. It was, after all, not very likely that he would ever return, nor would his son-in-law, Constantijn Nobel, ever think of leaving the Indies, where he had been born and raised. The following morning at ten o'clock Bitter and his daughters reached the fleet, lying at anchor in St. Nicholas Bay at Bantam, and boarded the *Waalstroom*. Bitter had been appointed vice-admiral of the homeward-bound fleet. The admiral, Jacob Couper—Bitter's children had boarded at one time with his family—sailed on *'s Landts Welvaren*, a ship belonging to the Zeeland Chamber of the Dutch East India Company. The two gentlemen, mindful of the custom of travelers to present their family and friends with parrots and monkeys, had chosen very exotic gifts. Couper took along a Javanese dwarf, intending to make a gift of him to someone in Holland. He had been given the unfortunate fellow as a personal gift from Amangkurat II, ruler of the Kingdom of Mataram.[22] Bitter brought along a cassowary, a bird from the island of Ceram. The German Johan Wilhelm Vogel, who was also traveling on board the *Waalstroom*, gives a lively description of the ship's departure, which, owing to the large number of house pets and livestock for the kitchen, must have resembled Noah's ark. A favorite pastime of the crew during the long and boring voyage was secretly feeding burning coals from the galley to Bitter's cassowary, which would eat anything it could get hold of.[23]

At the last minute, the execution of the deportation order was nearly endangered by a freak accident. At Bantam a sudden squall wreaked havoc among the fleet. The *Waalstroom* was torn loose from her moorings and rammed the nearby *Goudestein*, which lost her bowsprit and part of her bow and was forced to return to Batavia. The *Waalstroom*, on the other hand, sustained only light damage and was able to depart with the other ships.

Bitter's journal of the homeward voyage is remarkable for its concise and cryptic entries.[24] For days in a row there are nothing but notes about the ship's progress: morning and afternoon, topsail breeze, cloudy skies, good weather, and so on. On 20 March the African continent was sighted, and the crew began to plumb the depths. Only on 29 March did they cast anchor in Table Bay. Scores of other ships lay at anchor there, and it was not until a full month later that the fleet—now extended to include eleven ships—continued on its way, and swiftly, according to Bitter's account: "violently rolling, swelling sea, topsail breeze…" Everything was going as it should. Not until 2 July does it become clear why Bitter fails to mention anything interesting in this journal: he refers to another volume (unfortunately lost) that was his "daily journal of everything," meaning all events and happenings.

Once in European waters it was decided to make a long detour and sail to the north of Ireland and Scotland to avoid the Dunkirk privateers. On 11 August the ships joined the convoy of Admiral Evertsen, which had been lying at anchor, waiting for the homeward-bound ships. Ten days later Bitter arrived at the Nieuwe Diep, between Texel and Den Helder, "for which God alone may take credit and must therefore be thanked."

Cornelia, "very sickly and accompanied by her son, the burgher Cornelis Cnoll and his family," had already boarded the homeward-bound ship *Eenhoorn* belonging to the Rotterdam Chamber on 15 December 1687. This ship was to sail alone to Cape Town and join the rest of the fleet there.[25] The *Eenhoorn* took a more tragic course than the *Waalstroom*. Cornelia's health was a constant worry to her family, and this had been her son's most important reason for accompanying her. He had come along to offer aid and comfort, impelled also by the necessity, if she were to die at sea, of doing everything he could to salvage his inheritance before Bitter could lay his hands on it.

Instead, the unexpected happened. Cornelia blossomed in the fresh sea air; Cornelis, on the other hand, became seriously ill. So ill, in fact, that he died within sight of Table Mountain, where he was buried several days later by his grief-stricken mother, his wife, and their two children.[26] Cornelia, inconsolable, was left with only her daughter-in-law and two grandchildren; she no longer had a strong shoulder to cry on.

Approaching the Dutch coast, the fleet split up. The *Eenhoorn* arrived at the mouth of the river Schelde on 10 August, but it took the *Waalstroom* and the other ships of the Amsterdam Chamber another ten days to reach Texel. This gave Cornelia a slight edge on her husband, and she lost no time in taking advantage of it.

CHAPTER TEN

The Bitter End

May I find peace in the
heavenly glory above,
Amen.
—Johan Bitter[1]

Upon landing on the island of Walcheren, Cornelia van Nijen-roode left posthaste for The Hague to find Adriaen van Sterre-velt, the lawyer who had pleaded her case before the Court of Holland in 1682. After discussing the matter, they decided to follow the advice Cornelia had received from the High Government before leaving Batavia. The Governor-General and Councilors had decided that "to avoid further difficulties they did not want to take it upon themselves to delve into the matter of her rights, but, without prejudicing her case, to leave it up to her to proceed as advised in the fatherland." Cornelia and her lawyer decided to petition the provincial Court of Holland to issue a warrant for Johan Bitter's arrest, to be served without previous notice.

Johan Bitter was surprised upon his arrival in Amsterdam to hear of this swift action, but he countered by hurrying off to Gelderland, his native province, where he instituted proceedings against his wife at the provincial court. He was doubtless counting on the partiality of the

A man and a woman being committed to debtors' prison. Both Johan Bitter and his wife were detained in custody in the Castellenije at The Hague. (*Nederlandse Historieprenten (1550-1900) Platen-Atlas*, Amsterdam 1910)

local magistrates, but for once he was badly mistaken: without thinking, he went to Holland to settle some business and was promptly arrested at the instigation of Van Sterrevelt, who had been keeping an eye on him.

Bitter was locked up in the Castellenije, the "sponging house" —a preliminary detention center for debtors—of the court at The Hague.[2] These were reasonably comfortable quarters where debtors of a certain standing were detained until their cases were tried. Van Sterrevelt had been able to press for Bitter's arrest because Dutch law dictated that a debtor who resided outside the court's jurisdiction could be arrested upon entering the territory under its jurisdiction.[3] Normally the defendant would be freed immediately upon payment of bail, but Bitter, obstinate as usual, refused to pay it. He protested, saying that he had been unlawfully detained, because he had petitioned the court in Gelderland for an order to move the proceedings, and this had subsequently been granted. He proposed a plea of disqualification, in other words a motion contesting the court's jurisdiction, and suggested referring the matter to the provincial court of Gelderland, thereby forcing the court at The Hague to pass judgment. Having thus set the wheels of justice in motion, he coolly paid out the money and was released on bail.

On 11 November 1688 the court held a hearing, dismissed the defense's plea of disqualification, and ordered Bitter to answer the questions put to him and also to pay all expenses incurred. This was not at all what Bitter had been hoping for, and he subsequently lodged an appeal at the High Court of Holland, where he dished up the same arguments he had served to the provincial court.[4]

Alarmed by this legal tug-of-war and forewarned by letters from the Indies, the High Court appointed two deputies, Thomas Hope and Vincent Bronckhorst, to calm things down and come up with a proposal acceptable to both parties as to the path the proceedings should now take. This goal was achieved with remarkable swiftness. The lawyers agreed to "withdraw and terminate" all objections they had raised at the provincial courts of Holland and Gelderland, "to prepare the main case for the High Court," and "to bring all their problems and disputes, without previous notice, to the High Court." Both parties were given the right to take any kind of legal action they wished, with the understanding that Bitter's arrest at the provincial court of Holland would remain in force.[5]

Both parties then leapt into action and served a summons on each other. On behalf of Cornelia van Nijenroode, Adriaen van Sterrevelt requested a legal separation "from bed and board" (quo ad thorum et mensam) and demanded the restitution of 45,500 rixdollars and two stuivers, the proceeds of the public sale of the gold, silver, household effects, and slaves, including interest, as well as the 8,000 rixdollars that were still deposited with the Company.

George Roosenboom, the lawyer acting on behalf of Johan Bitter, demanded that Cornelia again take up residence with his client and that she disclose the full extent of her fortune, arguing that his client, as her guardian, was entitled to half her income and the right to manage her assets. If Cornelia should refuse to live with her husband, Bitter's lawyer asked that she be branded a "malicious deserter." He also asked the court to determine a "moderate" allowance which Bitter would then give to Cornelia to cover her living expenses. Furthermore, Roosenboom demanded compensation for the losses sustained by his client in this protracted affair, referring to the costly trip to the Indies that Bitter had been forced to undertake in order to lodge an appeal.[6]

The trial itself does not require lengthy treatment. In his dramatic opening statement, Van Sterrevelt painted a portrait of the marriage, the marital spats, and the subsequent legal disputes, whereupon George Roosenboom gave Bitter's version of events. After Roosenboom it was again Van Sterrevelt's turn. He stated that he found the cross-petition and the plaintiff's claims "filled with so many lies, impertinences, and malicious insinuations derived from such untrue and irrelevant assertions that it would be too tedious to produce them all in writing." He did, however, want to point out to the court that the concluding section of his opponent's claim clearly showed that he "has indulged his irascible and mercurial temper to such an extent as to demand an annulment of the marriage."[7]

Roosenboom made a concluding statement as well, dividing Cornelia's accusations, for the sake of convenience, into no fewer than a thousand articles, some of which he singled out for elucidation. To the reproach that Bitter had married her for her money, he replied that Bitter had "even made love to her as a good Christian husband should." To Cornelia's comments about the boastful letters he had written to his friends, he remarked that "this *Cato censorius* should ask herself whether she has ever discussed droll subjects with her friends or written letters with broadly humorous passages." Regarding the alleged squandering of her fortune, Roosenboom confirmed that Bitter had in fact spent a lot of money after his wife had run away from home, "having a very large and troublesome *familia* of forty or more slaves, as well as a coach and horses, altogether an extremely costly household to maintain." With respect to both their dispositions, he remarked that his client was "pious, honest, decent, and peace-loving . . . no squanderer or spendthrift," whereas his wife was "extremely irritable, nasty, and vicious."[8]

The court passed judgment on 4 July 1691. After thirteen years of fighting, the decision must have been a great disappointment to Cornelia: she was ordered "to return to her husband and live with him in peace and the fear of God." Bitter, the court ruled, was entitled to half his wife's income and usufructuary rights to her assets. Both parties were ordered to produce a declaration specifying their possessions—if necessary sealed under oath—to comply with these orders within two weeks, and to appear again in court on 17 July 1691.

From the edict issued on 1 December of that year, it appears that Cornelia still had a will of iron. Having refused to comply with the order of the High Court, it was now her turn to be detained in the Castellenije until she decided to relent.[9] She was soon released on bail, however, after handing over several inventories of her possessions, but another edict dated 24 July 1692 shows that both the court and her husband were convinced she was withholding information.

The High Court ruled, further to the judgments pronounced on 9 May 1684 and 4 July 1691, that Bitter had the right to manage and dispose of the goods in his wife's possession. Nonetheless, the court was not yet able to settle the couple's dispute as to the completeness of the lists and inventories they had submitted as a result of the 4 July 1691 ruling. The court declared the sequestration justified, gave Bitter permission to withdraw the 8,000 rixdollars that were deposited in the Company's treasury, and handed over to him the entire proceeds from the auction in Batavia. After the summer recess in August, Cornelia van Nijenroode and Johan Bitter were ordered to appear before the court again in September to settle the last differences regarding their respective inventories.[10]

This meeting never took place. Cornelia failed to show up, which means she must have died in the intervening period. Combing through the notarial documents in the municipal archives of Amsterdam, Vianen, and The Hague has brought nothing to light concerning the circumstances of her death, nor is there any mention of a last will and testament. Whether Cornelia died of exhaustion or chose to put an end to a life of humiliation and suffering, as her Japanese ancestors might have done, is something we will never know. Perhaps after all it is fitting for our tragic heroine not to die but simply to fade away.

Final Act

Before we attempt to draw any conclusions from this colonial drama we still have some loose ends to tie up. What finally happened to Bitter? Did he lapse into a long and happy old age, a living example of the saying that one man's meat is another man's poison?

It is not clear why Bitter took up residence in Wijk bij Duurstede, a town where he had no family. It is likely, however, that Nicolaas Schagen, vice-president of the Court of Justice at Batavia and a member of the Wijk patriciate, introduced his friend Bitter to his native town.[11] At all events, any visitor to this pretty town would agree with Bitter that he could have chosen no better place to spend the autumn of his life.

The last couple of centuries have seen only minor changes in the town. Duurstede Castle, of which only ruins remain, was already crumbling in Bitter's day. The apple orchards that burgomaster Bitter loved so well have made way for the present mayor's pride and joy: an industrial park.

The local, administrative, and family archives housed in the Utrecht State Archives, as well as a case study on the regents of Wijk bij Duurstede, have yielded interesting information on the subsequent course of Bitter's life.[12]

On 27 June 1692 three new members were admitted to the congregation of the Reformed Church in Wijk bij Duurstede: the lawyer Johan Bitter and his daughters Aletta and Eva.[13] At this time four of Bitter's children were still alive: Bartha, the eldest, was married to Constantijn Nobel, Jr. and living in Batavia. Arnolt was working as a lawyer somewhere in Holland and did not become a member of the church in Wijk bij Duurstede until 1696. Aletta and Eva, who had returned to Holland with Johan Bitter on board the *Waalstroom*, were still unmarried and living with their father. Shortly after his arrival in Wijk bij Duurstede, Bitter bought a house on Oeverstraat.[14]

The exact location of Bitter's house is no longer known, but the few stately patrician homes still standing bear witness to what the street, which crosses the town from north to south, must once have been. Near the southern end of the street lies the former Leuterpoort, the town gate now called the Runmolenpoort. The marketplace in the center of town is only a two-minute walk from Oeverstraat. An imposing church tower rises above the town hall, which was built in 1662. Bitter's coat of arms, which once adorned the wall of the church, has disappeared.[15]

From the time of his arrival in Wijk bij Duurstede, all of Bitter's actions indicate his firm intention to use the rich gifts bestowed on him by his second marriage to ensure himself of an agreeable and tranquil old age. Although this had certainly been his plan, his life in Wijk was soon filled with activity. Within three years Bitter occupied a seat on the town council, where he continued to play a prominent role for the next twenty years. He finally died on 17 March 1714, nearly seventy-five years of age.[16]

Johan Bitter sat on the Bench of Aldermen four times and served as burgomaster of Wijk twice. This pattern is typical of the times. In the second half of the seventeenth century it became increasingly common for retired men to occupy seats on the town council. In a city like Hoorn, for example, 20,000 guilders were enough to ensure one of an oligarch's lifestyle.[17] The 8,000 rixdollars that the High Court had awarded to Bitter were already enough to guarantee his success.

Bitter was not a man blessed with tact, and he often let his temper get the better of him. One account has it that the 63-year-old Bitter, then serving as burgomaster, was regularly at odds with an alderman forty years his junior, a certain Mr. Vosch whom Bitter persisted in calling "young man." Vosch got so fed up with Bitter's patronizing ways that one day he asked him if he was familiar with the Spanish saying that a young stallion was worth more than an old mule. It was all the other aldermen could do to keep Bitter from whacking his younger colleague with his cane.[18] On another occasion several members of the town council sent a list of complaints to the States of Utrecht to illustrate the disdain with which Bitter treated his fellow regents.[19]

Johan Bitter's daughters were well on their way to becoming old spinsters when Bitter finally succeeded in marrying them off to members of well-to-do regents' families in other towns. Fat Eva married Hendrick Both, the equally obese burgomaster of Amersfoort who was descended from the first Governor-General of the Indies, Pieter Both.[20] In 1707 Aletta married Albert van Lidth de Jeude of Tiel, but she died less than a year later.[21] Arnolt returned to the Indies in 1703, where he eventually rose to the office of public prosecutor of the Dutch East India Company.[22]

Johan Bitter remained single, but in spite of this—or perhaps because of it—he had an agreeable family life. Not only did his daughters live with him for many years, but he also enjoyed the company of a nephew, Pieter Nobel, who came to board with him in 1694, and later on his grandsons, Johan and Dirk Nobel, who were entrusted to his care by his daughter Bartha.[23] Several letters from Bartha and Arnolt to their father have been preserved in the Utrecht State Archives, and these epistles testify not only to the warmth and affection between Bitter and his brood but also to the esteem in which his children held him. The tone of these letters broadens our picture of Johan Bitter, whose children worshipped him as a good father who could always be counted on to lend them a sympathetic ear.[24]

In her letter of 20 November 1701, Bartha writes of the death of her husband, Constantijn Nobel, and hints at her misgivings about living in Batavia as a widow, her apprehension being all the greater because she and her husband "had sustained great [financial] losses several years back," so that she "did not have the funds she might otherwise have had." This letter sheds light on the especially close bond between father and daughter. She thanks her father for all his letters and also for a particularly kind gesture: three small portraits he had sent to Batavia. The likenesses of her sons Johan and Dirk clearly showed "the charming change" undergone by her boys in Holland, while the portrait of Papa showed "how little [he] had changed, only the gray hair, but for the rest [he] looked better than ever." What had touched Bartha most in her father's last letter was his account of the arrival in Wijk bij Duurstede of ten-year-old Dirk, who had come to meet "his grandfather whom he had never seen before. The tender and moving words of Your Worship's account of this" had moved her greatly. Bartha asked her father to break the sad news of their father's death to her sons. She could not as yet say what the future would bring, but she dreaded living on her own:

> Meanwhile I am here alone and have no one at all to comfort me except my son Constant. But because one cannot oppose God's will, which is always good and holy—no matter how hard it is to bear— I shall patiently submit to it in the faith that the Lord God will not forsake me and will again bless me and my dear children, that they may become upright and God-fearing men. . . .

Bartha took comfort in the thought that her brother Arnolt would perhaps move back to the East. Her wish eventually came true. Shortly after his arrival she married for the second time; her new husband was the Company merchant Andries Leendertszoon. It was not until 1711 that Bartha and her husband began to make serious plans to return to Holland, where she hoped to embrace her father and her two grown-up sons, (one of whom had died, but the news of his death had not yet reached her).

The Balance

At this point it is worthwhile dwelling for a minute on Bartha's remarks about her family's financial situation. Shortly before his death Bartha's husband lost a great deal of money in a business venture, but luckily she still had enough to live on, thanks to the income from some houses she rented out. In her letter she also refers to bills of exchange she had sent her father in Holland, a fact confirmed by archival documents in both Wijk bij Duurstede and Amsterdam.[25] In a genealogical study of the Nobel family the financial position of Bartha's children was thoroughly researched. The education of Bartha's sons was financed by a special fund of 8,000 rixdollars left to them by an uncle, Jacobus Nobel. Surprisingly, it also emerged that by 1711 Johan Bitter was indebted to Bartha and her husband to the tune of 25,325 rixdollars. Did this mean that the old man was still in the habit of squandering money?[26]

One cannot help thinking that Bitter had appropriated funds for his own use from the money he was keeping for his children and grand-children. Apart from the bills of exchange, the records of the notary Nicolaes Keppel prove that Bitter also managed the assets of his son Arnolt. In July 1698 he was appointed his son's proxy in all affairs.[27]

As it turns out, Bitter succeeded in hanging on to much less money from his marriage to Cornelia van Nijenroode than one would expect. Lawsuits and lawyers have their price. Moreover, bearing in mind the terms of the marriage settlement, since all of Cornelia's children had died, her grandchildren were her heirs *in loco parentis*. Finally, Cornelia would certainly have avoided mentioning the name Bitter in her will. This means that after Cornelia's death Bitter was forced to turn over all her possessions to the children of her son, Cornelis.

The supposition that in the end Bitter did not actually make very much money out of Cornelia is strengthened by information from the Amsterdam municipal archives. The register of guardianships of the Amsterdam Orphans' Chamber records that on 25 January 1689 a certain Abraham van Uylenbroeck was appointed legal guardian of Cornelis Cnoll's children: Anna, six, and Jacobus Wijbrant Cnoll, two and a half. By checking the register of contributions made to the Orphans' Chamber (in other words, its incoming capital), it was ascertained that Cornelis Cnoll left 56,700 rixdollars in bills of exchange to his wife and children, along with a lot of curiosa and other possessions. In the spring of 1690 Hillegonda Dubbeldecop bought her children's share of the porcelain and jewelry for 15,734 guilders, which means that Cornelis Cnoll's estate was worth at least 150,000 guilders. Two years later Hillegonda appeared again at the Orphans' Chamber, accompanied by her prospective second husband, Alexander Henderson. The day before, she had transferred the guardianship of her two children to him in the presence of the notary Jacobus van Uylenbroeck.[28]

These details explain the only reference to Cornelia's will that has so far been uncovered,[29] the gist of which reads as follows: "Johan Bitter testifies that he has reached an agreement with Messrs. Alexander Henderson and Abraham Uylenbroeck concerning their dispute about the estate belonging to him and his late wife. Under the terms of the agreement, a certain bill of exchange worth 6,104 rixdollars that was sent from the Indies while his wife was still alive and was never cashed will become the property of the above-mentioned gentlemen." Clearly, Bitter felt the guardian of the Cnoll children breathing down his neck.

Cornelia's grandson, Jacobus Wijbrandt Cnoll, would derive little pleasure from his large inheritance. He died in Vianen in September

1703 at the age of seventeen, leaving 122,000 guilders to his sister Anna and her husband Christiaan van Schillebeecq.[30] Jacobus Wijbrandt, who boarded in Vianen with two old spinsters, Anna and Petronella Losser, must have been a regular visitor to the home of Reverend François Caron, who was the preacher in nearby Lexmond. Also a product of the union between a prominent Company employee and a Japanese woman from Hirado, Caron had been one of Cornelia's playmates. Reverend Caron took pity on young Jacobus and frequently cheered him up with stories about his father, grandmother, and great-grandparents in far-off Asia.

In the final analysis, we may say with reasonable certainty that the lion's share of Pieter Cnoll's estate did not fall into Johan Bitter's hands. He therefore had to be content with the considerable sums he had managed to spirit away while Cornelia was still alive.

Epilogue

We now return to that spring evening in 1712, when we first met burgo-master Bitter in his apple orchard behind the Bemmel Dike. He is still seated on the bench in front of his garden house. While one white petal after another flutters down around him, Johan Bitter continues to pore over his son's letter. What was Arnolt going on about now?

> But how people tire themselves worrying about things temporal! What useless and vain thoughts we have about our well-being in this world, where everything is pure vanity. For just when we think we have risen above the world's cares and can spend the rest of our days in peace and tranquility, death comes to snatch us away.

"Why all this philosophizing?" muttered father Johan, "my Arnolt isn't like this. What has gotten into him over there in the tropics? And what does 'sister Leendertszoon,' my Bartha, have to do with it?"

Let us take sister Leendertszoon as an example. Last year she was
filled with such a passionate longing for our fatherland, where she
hoped to find pleasure in the company of her old father, her sons,
and other relatives. Yet, to my deep regret, on Sunday in the early
morning hours, after the church bells tolled five o'clock, Almighty
God saw fit to take her from us to Heaven above, where, I hope, her
soul may rest in peace with God and she may delight in eternal bliss.

Only three years ago you, dear father, had four children who were
all leading decent and respectable lives. Since that time their number has been reduced by half.

*Johan Bitter went pale as his glassy eyes skimmed the rest of the letter. His
hands shaking, he laid the letter on his knees. Bartha, for whom he'd been
waiting all these years. Bartha, who knew everything about his life in the
Indies from the beginning to the end, who had been his help and stay since the
death of her mother on that fateful first voyage. Bartha, whose two sons he
had raised himself; he had even carried one of them, little Johan, to his grave
two years ago. Bartha, the only one he could have shared his memories with.
Bartha, his Bartha, was dead.*

Afterword

History is the history of success,
but biographies don't make this distinction.
—Richard Holmes

Three hundred years after the High Court passed judgment, this tragic story was resurrected from the archives and recorded for the pleasure and edification of the modern-day reader. By some quirk of fate—or perhaps the intervention of Clio, the muse of history—two people were driven into each other's arms, though they did not seem to suit each other in the slightest: the country gentleman Johan Bitter and the "Company child" Cornelia van Nijenroode. Although they lived three centuries ago in the colonial city of Batavia, they are not so far removed from us that we cannot follow the motives behind much of what they did and said. In the course of this biographical study we have seen to what extent the unhappy couple's thoughts and actions were held in check by the reins of social control prevailing at the time, including the administration of justice, the attendance of collective rituals such as the Lord's Supper, and the interference of the ubiquitous Dutch East India Company. All this forms the backdrop to a human drama, but equally important is the fact that "in a biography you see people wrestling with the same problems we have: lovesickness, failed marriages, unfulfilled ambitions, and so on."[1]

Though the moral of this story is timeless—when a woman makes a man rich, the result is discord and disdain (according to Father Cats)[2]—the story itself is time-bound, for the position of the "Batavian widow" changed after 1700, when money and power in Batavia increasingly came to be held by a small number of established families. Extensive landownership and access to the most lucrative positions within the Company enabled them to develop into the local patrician class.[3] Male relatives could exercise a great deal of pressure on greedy outsiders who courted a wealthy female in their family, threatening her interests as well as their own. As Arnolt Bitter related in his letter to his father, around the turn of the century there were scarcely any more rich widows to be found in Batavia.

The story of Johan Bitter and Cornelia van Nijenroode is significant because it constitutes a test case, showing what could happen when both partners had recourse to a whole range of legal weapons but no relatives to lend them a helping hand. The administration of justice is supposed to be based on fair play and impartiality, but such concepts were flouted in seventeenth-century Batavia. It would not be fair, however, to judge the actions of our ancestors by our own standards, though we cannot deny that the administration of justice in the seventeenth century ran a curious course, and not only in the Asian colonies where the Dutch East India Company held sway.

Several prominent historians have pronounced judgment on the seventeenth-century judicial process. Fockema Andreae, for example, called this turbulent period "a paradise for lawyers."[4] One only has to look at Bitter to see how much he felt at ease in the Dutch judicial system, which offered ample scope for legal chicanery. Van Deursen states that it was pointless for the average citizen to institute legal proceedings against a regent.[5] As supporting evidence he quotes Roorda, who shows how, in the days of the Dutch Republic, a difficult person could simply be banned from the city without due process of law: "This was exacerbated by the fact that in the cities the relations between judges and political leaders were too close."[6]

Clearly, a matrimonial law stipulating that a wife's assets automatically belonged to her husband—even if she had inherited or earned those assets herself—left little room for an ill-treated wife to take action against a grasping husband, especially because, legally speaking, she and he were one and the same person.

In his treatise on "The Subjection of Women," John Stuart Mill clearly describes the issue of property rights as regards a married couple.

> She can acquire no property but for him; the instant it becomes hers, even if by inheritance, it becomes ipso facto his... By means of settlement, the rich usually contrive to withdraw the whole or part of the inherited property of the wife from the absolute control of the husband: but they do not succeed in keeping it under her own control; the utmost they can do only prevents the husband from squandering it, at the same time debarring the rightful owner from its use.[7]

The stringent marriage settlements Mill refers to did not become common in England until after 1700, but such settlements could be quite effective in preventing a husband from disposing of his wife's assets.[8]

This case clearly demonstrates the weak legal position of women in the Netherlands, but how were women actually treated? Cornelia van Nijenroode had a marriage settlement drawn up, as was customary in her time, but problems arose right from the beginning because the settlement did not disclose the full extent of her assets. When the contract was actually put to the test, it proved to be full of loopholes, not only because the law gave her husband the right to manage her property, but also because her husband suspected—not unreasonably—that part of the assets he was supposed to be managing were being concealed from him.

We can only guess at the reasons for such secretiveness, although one motive seems obvious: Pieter Cnoll, in his capacity as first head merchant of Batavia Castle, had earned enough on the side to amass a great fortune in a relatively short time. No doubt his quick-witted wife had "aided and abetted" him in his "extracurricular" activities. After Pieter Cnoll's death, it was not in Cornelia's interest to disclose the full value of his estate. She knew all too well what the consequences might be; after all, her father's entire estate had been confiscated on the grounds that it had been acquired through private trade. Determined not to be taken advantage of, Cornelia protested loudly when she caught her second husband misappropriating her assets. When hostilities escalated, mutual friends tried to step in, and when their attempts at mediation failed it was the church's turn to intervene. The rules laid down by the church, however, were aimed more at safeguarding collective rituals such as the Lord's Supper than at mediating between individual members of the congregation.

That Cornelia initially gained the upper hand in this conflict was due to the discovery of Bitter's diamond smuggling, at which time the Company directors in Holland ordered the High Government in Batavia to take immediate legal action against Johan Bitter and send him home as an "employee useless to the Company." In other words, Bitter, accused of engaging in private trade, was placed outside the law by the Heren XVII. Only under such circumstances could the judges in Batavia—after first sentencing Bitter in the smuggling case—find the courage to grant Cornelia special privileges: she succeeded in obtaining a provisional separation and escaped having to accompany her husband to Holland. Altogether this was a clear sign that in those days the executive and the judiciary were working hand in glove. To be sure, Cornelia was instructed on this occasion to disclose the full amount of her fortune, but this court ruling ran counter to her late husband's will, and, as we have seen, Cornelia would not budge an inch. The thread running through this entire story is in fact Cornelia's steadfast refusal to reveal the true extent of her assets.

After his forced repatriation to Holland, Johan Bitter brazened it out, persuading the Company directors to admit that they had dealt with him—a Company employee—so severely that his personal interests were seriously prejudiced. The Heren XVII subsequently advised the Governor-General in Batavia to give Bitter permission, which had at first been denied, to request a review of his case, although in doing so they were actually violating their own rules. After returning to Batavia, Bitter so scandalously abused his privileged position as a member of the Court of Justice that the Court itself was finally unable to mediate in the case, let alone sit in judgment. This prompted Governor-General Camphuys to brand the affair a threat to public order. From this time on, the marriage was an administrative—or, to use the terminology of the time, a political—matter. This procedure, turning what was in theory a purely legal problem into a political issue, was often implemented in later years and met with the tacit approval of the Heren XVII. However, even the Governor-General's personal intervention could not bring about a truce. In other words, Batavian society did not have the means to put its own house in order.

The course taken by the proceedings in Holland speaks for itself. The formality, not to say rigidity, with which the law was upheld is more reminiscent of the relentless fury of the Fates in a Greek drama than of the actions of judges in a country that prided itself on being open-minded. Where was the generosity of spirit that the nineteenth-century Dutch poet Everhardus Johannes Potgieter admired so much in his oft-quoted lines on the fatherland?

> Stay what you were, when in triumph you shone:
> Make Europe recognize its seat of order,
> Let the oppressed call thee refuge and home,
> Land of my fathers, my glory, my own![9]

Now it is time to take a last look at Cornelia. Was she a Madame Butterfly left in the lurch by a Dutch lawyer? Or did she resemble the female praying mantis, who eats the male after mating? Her dogged struggle, reminiscent of a valiant samurai fighting for a lost but honorable cause, recalls that odd yet apposite word used in Nagasaki to describe a strong-willed woman: *otemba*.

Notes

Abbreviations used in endnotes:

ARA = Algemeen Rijksarchief (General State Archives)

VOC = Verenigde Oostindische Compagnie (Dutch East India Company)

RU = Rijksarchief Utrecht (Utrecht State Archives)

HR = Hoge Raad (Supreme Court [of Holland and Zeeland])

GA = Gemeentearchief Amsterdam (Amsterdam Municipal Archives)

GG = Governor-General

Notes to Chapter One
OTEMBA

1. RU, "Archieven van de Familie van Boetzelaer, 1316–1952" (Van Boetzelaer family archives), no. 483.
2. Ibid.
3. Hugo de Groot (Hugo Grotius), *Inleidinge tot de Hollandsche Rechts-Geleerdheid*, University Press, Leiden 1965 (2nd edition), including the corrections, additions, and comments supplied by the writer (found in the Lund edition), with references to his other writings, publication of commentary, and appendixes provided by F. Dovring, H. F. W. D. Fischer, and E. M. Meijers. I. 5,19.
4. H. de Groot, *Inleidinge*. I. 5, 21.
5. File on David van Lennep 1771–1804, collection of manuscripts in the Maritiem Museum Prins Hendrik, Rotterdam.
6. H. T. Colenbrander (ed.), *Jan Pieterszoon Coen; Bescheiden omtrent zijn verblijf in Indië* (The Hague 1919), I, 644.
7. *Patriase missive* of 31 August 1643 in H 54, KITLV manuscript collection, Leiden.

8. Nicolaus de Graaff, *Oost-Indise Spiegel*, published by J. C. M. Wansinck, Linschoten Vereeniging, vol. 33 (The Hague 1930), 30.

9. Jean Baptiste Tavernier, *De Zes Reizen van de Heer J. Bapt. Tavernier* (Amsterdam 1682), 262.

10. J. Crawford, *History of the Indian Archipelago* (London 1820), I, 147.

Notes to Chapter Two
PERIOD PIECE

1. *Journalen van de gedenkwaardige reysen van Willem Ysbrantszoon. Bontekoe, 1618–1625*, Linschoten Vereeniging, no. LIV, The Hague 1952.

2. ARA, VOC 1110, fols. 386–400.

3. ARA, Eerste afdeling, aanwinsten 1886 A.V. (K.A.) 225, missive 20 November 1637, "licentie van 't vertreck der Nederlantsche kinderen."

Notes to Chapter Three
PORTRAIT OF A MARRIAGE

1. Elias Hesse, *Gold-Bergwerke in Sumatra, 1680–1683* (The Hague 1931), 110.

2. Iwao Seiichi, "Kapitain no musume Cornelia no shogai" (The life of Cornelia, daughter of the captain), in *Rekishi to jinbutsu* (Tokyo 1978), 149.

3. Her first husband, whom she married in 1644, was an English lieutenant named Michael Tresoir. After his death in 1659 she married Abelis Benting, with whom she had a son, Johan.

4. Iwao Seiichi, "The life of Pieter Hartsinck, the Japanner (1637–1680); 'grand-pupil' of Descartes," in *The Transactions of the Asiatic Society of Japan*, Third Series, XX (1985), 145–167.

5. *Daghregister gehouden in 't casteel Batavia. Anno 1682*, Batavia 1931, 1076.

6. W. Ph. Coolhaas (ed.), *Generale Missiven van Gouverneurs-Generaal en Raden aan Heren XVII der Verenigde Oostindische Compagnie* (The Hague 1960), I, 640.

7. Pieter van Hoorn, "Praeparatoire consideratiën," in J. K. J. de Jonge, *Opkomst van het Nederlandsch gezag in Oost-Indië* (The Hague 1872), VI, 130.

8. F. de Haan, *Oud Batavia* (Batavia 1922), I, 248.

9. Iwao Seiichi, "Japanese emigrants in Batavia during the 17th century," in *Acta Asiatica* 18 (1978), 150. A few of these letters have been preserved in the prefectural library of Nagasaki. See Murakami Naojiro, *Boekishi-jo no Hirado* [Hirado in the history of trade] (Tokyo 1917), 21–27.

10. Sato Dokusho, "Jagatara-bun no shin hakken" [A newly discovered Jakarta writing], in *Rekishi Chiri* 16 (1910), 75–81, 164–175, 472–485.

11. Hamada Sukeeimon was a Japanese Christian from Nagasaki, who lived in Batavia. In Dutch sources he is called Jan. Yoshitsugi Kuzaeimon was the younger brother of Hamada's wife (Iwao, "Kapitan no musume Cornelia no shogai," in *Rekishi to Jinbutsu*, 151).

12. J. A. van der Chijs, *Nederlandsch-Indisch Plakaatboek 1602–1811* (Batavia 1886) II: 509, "Voorschrift nopens de goederen, welke naar Japan niet mogen medegenomen worden," 18 April 1670.

13. Concerning the instructions of senior merchants, see *Plakaatboek* II: 80–5, 214–7, 380, 398; 9 April 1644, 11 February 1656, 25 November 1664, and 22 September 1665.

14. *Plakaatboek* II: 380.

15. See *Daghregister* 1666: 80 (4 June). A summary of Pieter Cnoll's career is to be found in the index of persons (listed alphabetically) in the minutes of the proceedings of the High Government (Resoluties GG en Raad)(ARA, VOC 828).

16. Arsip Nasional, notarial archives Huysman, 15 February 1672, fol. 22, "Testament tusschen de heer Pieter Cnoll van Delft, eerste oppercoopman dezes casteels ende d'eerbare juffrouw Cornelia van Nieuwenroode geboortigh van Hirando in Japan, echteman en vrouw." A copy of this will was given to me in 1975 by Prof. Iwao Seiichi in Tokyo.

17. This decision played an important role in later developments. As long as there was no reliable inventory, it was easy for the contending parties to be at loggerheads. The lack of an inventory means that it was impossible to ascertain how rich Cnoll really was. A contemporary of Pieter Cnoll, Georg Meister, estimated Cnoll's fortune at "20 Tonnen Goldes." See *Der Orientalisch-Indianische Kunst- und Lust-Gärtner etc.* (Dresden 1692), 293.

18. *Plakaatboek* II: 457, fol. 24.
19. She would remain their legal guardian until she remarried, after which her guardianship would be transferred to her new husband or a specially appointed guardian; see Hugo de Groot, *Inleidinge*, I. 7,11.
20. *Daghregister* 1672: 53.
21. See Georg Meister, *Orientalisch-Indianische Reise*, 293.

Notes to Chapter Four
SETTING THE SCENE

1. F. W. Stapel (ed.), *Pieter van Dam, beschrijvinge van de Oostindische Compagnie* (The Hague 1927–1943) I, 244.
2. ARA, VOC 107, 3 November 1673.
3. This information comes from the "Genealogische aantekeningen over verwante families" in the Van Boetzelaer family archives, RU, no. 6.
4. The *Album Promotorum* mentions this event on 16 February 1662: "Johannes Bitter Arenaco-Gelrus, post habitam publicam disputationem in conclavi promotus, promotere d. Arnoldo Schonaeo." See O. Schutte, *Het Album Promotorum van de academie te Harderwijk* (Arnhem 1980), 23.
5. J. la Bree, *De rechterlijke organisatie en rechtsbedeling te Batavia in de 17e eeuw* (Rotterdam 1951), 54.
6. J. la Bree, *De rechterlijke organisatie* and J. van Kan, "Het rechtsmiddel der revisie voor den Raad van Justitie des kasteels Batavia" in *BKI* 102, 1–40.
7. La Bree, *De rechterlijke organisatie*, 54.
8. Femme Gaastra, *Bewind en Beleid bij de VOC 1672–1701* (Zutphen 1989), 37; ARA, VOC 239, 15 November 1673.
9. Ibid.
10. J. R. Bruijn, F. S. Gaastra, and I. Schöffer (eds.), *Dutch Asiatic Shipping in the 17th and 18th Centuries*, II (The Hague 1979), 184.
11. F. van der Burg, *Curieuse Beschrijving van de Gelegentheid, Zeden, Godsdienst en ommegang, van verscheyden Oost-Indische Gewesten en machtige landschappen* (Rotterdam 1677), 14.
12. ARA, HR (Holland and Zeeland), 783, fol. 63.
13. Ibid.
14. C. R. Boxer, *Mary and Misogyny, Women in Iberian Expansion Overseas*

1415–1815: Some Facts, Fancies and Personalities (London 1975), 48.

15. Ibid., 78.
16. HR 783, fol. 63.
17. Hugo de Groot, *Inleidinge*, I. 5, 23.
18. A. S. de Blécourt and H. F. W. D. Fischer, *Kort begrip van het oud-vaderlandsch burgerlijk recht* (The Hague 1967), 70.
19. ARA, HR 783, fol. 64.
20. RU, Van Boetzelaer family archives, inv. no. 16.

Notes to Chapter Five
GIVE AND TAKE

1. Als de most, te nauw bedwongen / Leit en worstelt, leit en zucht / Zonder adem, zonder lucht, / Ziet dan doet hij vreemde sprongen / Ziet, dan riekt de ganse vloer / Na de dampen van de moer. Poem titled "Invisa nemo imperia retinuit diu (Een rijk van dwang en duurt niet lang)," from "Emblemata moralia et oeconomica" (1627), in *Alle de Wercken van den Heere Jacob Cats*, Amsterdam 1712.
2. ARA, HR 783, fol. 84.
3. F. Valentijn, *Oud en Nieuw Oost-Indiën etc.* IV–1 (Dordrecht/Amsterdam 1726), 385.
4. ARA, HR 783, fol. 65.
5. ARA, HR 783, fol. 85.
6. ARA, HR 783, fol. 65v.
7. On 15 September 1676.
8. ARA, HR 783, fol. 65.
9. ARA, HR 783, fol. 66.
10. ARA, HR 783, fol. 94.
11. ARA, HR 783, fol. 85.
12. ARA, HR 783, fols. 66–67.
13. ARA, HR 783, fol. 67.
14. ARA, HR 783, fol. 85.
15. J. Mooij (ed.), *Bouwstoffen voor de geschiedenis der protestantsche kerken in Nederlandsch-Indië*, III (Weltevreden 1931), 303–304. See also A. Th. van Deursen, *Het kopergeld van de Gouden Eeuw*, IV (Assen 1980), 50.

16. Mooij, *Bouwstoffen*, III, 303–304.

17. ARA, HR 783, fols. 67v, 68.

18. ARA, HR 783, fols. 66v, 68.

19. *Daghregister* 1676: 356.

20. ARA, HR 783, fol. 69.

21. Mooij, *Bouwstoffen*, III, 326.

22. Mooij, *Bouwstoffen*, III, 329.

23. ARA, HR 783, fol. 69v.

24. Mooij, *Bouwstoffen*, III, 333.

25. Ibid., III, 340.

26. Ibid., III, 341, 342, 344.

27. Ibid., III, 360.

28. Ibid., III, 361.

29. Ibid., III, 366.

30. Ibid., III, 375–76.

31. There were two precedents with respect to this. The right of the church to enforce ecclesiastical discipline regularly led to conflicts with the civil authorities. Van Boetzelaer gives a good example of a reverend who was punished by the church council "before the judge had passed judgment in the case." C. W. Th. van Boetzelaer, baron of Asperen and Dubbeldam, *De protestantsche kerk in Nederlandsch-Indië; haar ontwikkeling van 1620–1939* (The Hague 1947), 72.

32. Mooij, *Bouwstoffen*, III, 386.

33. ARA, VOC 1431, fol. 766.

34. ARA, VOC 1431, fol. 766v.

35. In his article on Andreas Cleyer, De Haan, speaking of Speelman's speculative transactions, concludes that "the clever statesman, the bold and resolute admiral and field marshal, was also an inveterate cheat who would even stoop to base profiteering and swindling the natives." F. de Haan, "Uit oude notarispapieren II, Andreas Cleyer" in *TBG* 66 (1903), 442, 448.

36. F. Valentijn, *Oud en Nieuw Oost-Indiën* IV–1, 311.

37. ARA, VOC 1431, fol. 770.

Notes to Chapter Six
THE PARROT'S ACCOUNT

1. ARA, VOC 240, unfoliated.
2. See F. W. Stapel (ed.), *Pieter van Dam; Beschrijvinge van de Oostindische Compagnie* III (The Hague 1927–47), 383.
3. ARA, VOC 240, 29 July, 12 August, 26 August 1677.
4. ARA, VOC 108, meeting held on 8 September 1677.
5. Pieter van Dam devotes a chapter to the strictly forbidden private trade by employees of the Dutch East India Company. With regard to the diamond trade, he remarks that the Heren XVII never enforced a consistent policy on this score. F. W. Stapel, *Pieter van Dam. Beschrijvinge*, III, 384. Diamonds were always popular among smugglers owing to their small size and relatively great value. The large number of edicts and regulations (to be found in the *Realia* and *Plakaatboek*) banning the private trade in diamonds all testify to the incidence of Company employees engaging in such trade.
6. Willem van Alphen, secretary to the Court of Holland from 1631 to 1684, performed a great service to posterity by publishing in the *Papegaey* documents he found to be of an exemplary or unique nature. I made use of the 1683 edition.
7. Van Alphen, *Papegaey*, 10–14.
8. ARA, VOC 108, minutes of the meeting of the Heren XVII held on 8 September.
9. ARA, VOC 108, 8 September 1677.
10. *Daghregister* 1678: 291–295.
11. ARA, HR 783, fol. 70.
12. *Daghregister* 1679: 419.
13. L. J. van Apeldoorn, *Geschiedenis van het Nederlands huwelijksrecht voor de invoering van de Fransche wetgeving* (Amsterdam 1925), 197.
14. ARA, HR 783, fols. 70, 86.
15. Mooij, *Bouwstoffen*, III, 436.
16. *Daghregister* 1679: 509.
17. ARA, HR 783, fol. 87.
18. *Daghregister* 1679: 579, 16 February.
19. *Daghregister* 1680: 108, 12 March.
20. *Daghregister* 1680: 111.

21. Willem van Alphen, II, 313–327.
22. In the case of a hearing in the Dutch Republic a period of two weeks was usually allowed, this being extended to three weeks if the hearing was in Zeeland, because of poor traveling connections between the islands. See F. C. J. Ketelaar, "De procesgang bij het Hof van Holland, Zeeland en West-Friesland" in *Verslag en bijdragen van de Rijks Archiefschool, 1969–1970* (Utrecht 1971) with regard to the legal proceedings at the Court of Holland in the seventeenth century.
23. Van Alphen, *Papegaey*, II, 325.
24. Ibid., 327.
25. Pieter van Dam, *Beschrijvinge van de Oostindische Compagnie*, 7 vols., The Hague 1927–47.
26. Van Alphen, *Papegaey*, II, 317.
27. Ibid., 319.
28. Ibid., 318 (the text incorrectly mentions 24 March).

Notes to Chapter Seven
THE LOST SHEEP

1. ARA, HR, fol. 71.
2. 1631 *Generale missive* of the Heren XVII of 23 November 1631, 21 October 1676, and 1 November 1678.
3. 11 July 1680, *Plakaatboek* III, 47.
4. Mooij, *Bouwstoffen*, III, 456.
5. Ibid., 463.
6. *Daghregister* 1681: 483.
7. On 3 July 1681, when the church council again met to decide on the admittance or rejection of prospective communicants. *Daghregister* 1681: 483.
8. By chance the "Civiele Rolle" of 1681–1682 has been preserved in The Hague. The above-mentioned discussion and the contents of Bitter's letter are recorded therein. ARA, VOC 9236, 6 November 1681, fol. 151.
9. Van Alphen, *Papegaey*, II, 320–321.
10. Mooij, *Bouwstoffen*, III, 489.
11. Van Alphen, *Papegaey*, II, 322–323.
12. Ibid., 323.

13. ARA, VOC 109, Resoluties Heren XVII, 15 June 1682.
14. H. de Groot, *Inleidinge* I. 5, 20, "De onlusten lang duirend werd oock wel by 't gerecht toegestaen scheidinge van de by-wooning, den echt-band blijvende, ende met verstand dat altijd wederom getracht moet werden tot vereeniging."
15. Resoluties Heren XVII, ARA, VOC 106, 8 March 1683.
16. Van Kan, "Het rechtsmiddel der revisie," 1.
17. Pieter van Dam, who devotes a section to this phenomenon, counted hundreds of cases in his day. Stapel, *Pieter van Dam*, III, 96.
18. Ibid.
19. *Plakaatboek*, I, 512.
20. Van Kan, "Het rechtsmiddel der revisie," 27.

Notes to Chapter Eight
THE SO-CALLED RECONCILIATION

1. N. De Graaff, J. C. M. Warnsinck (ed.), *Reisen van Nicolaus de Graaff gedaan naar alle gewesten des werelds, beginnende 1639 tot 1687 incluis*, Linschoten Vereeniging 33 (The Hague 1930), 168–170. [Journal kept] on *'t Schip de Ridderschap van Hollandt* [Johan Bitter], 1683, Manuscript catalogue of the Rijksmuseum Nederlands Scheepvaartmuseum, I, 276.
2. Mooij, *Bouwstoffen*, III, 569.
3. Mooij, *Bouwstoffen*, III, 573, 9 December 1683.
4. Ibid., 574–575, 17 January 1684.
5. ARA, HR 783, fol. 88.
6. Stapel, "Speelman," 138.
7. Ibid., 141–142.
8. Valentijn, *Oud en nieuw*, IV, 315.
9. ARA, HR 783, fol. 88.
10. Mooij, *Bouwstoffen*, III, 611.
11. Ibid., 612.
12. ARA, HR 783, fol. 71.
13. ARA, HR 783, fol. 88.
14. ARA, HR 783, fols. 72, 89.
15. ARA, HR 783, fol. 72v.

16. See La Bree, *De rechterlijke organisatie*, 31–32; 53.
17. ARA, HR 783, fol. 73.
18. ARA, VOC 701, 1 May 1686.
19. ARA, VOC 701, Resoluties GG en Raad, 1 May 1686.
20. ARA, VOC 701, 14 June 1686, fols. 276–277.
21. ARA, VOC 701, 20 August 1686.
22. ARA, HR 783, fol. 74.
23. ARA, HR 783, fol. 75.
24. ARA, VOC 1418, fol. 452.
25. ARA, VOC 702, 15 January 1687.

Notes to Chapter Nine
THE LAST ROUND

1. ARA, VOC 693, 11 October 1678.
2. *Daghregister* 1680: 361, 618–620, 7–8 June.
3. ARA, VOC 783, fol. 89.
4. ARA, VOC 702, Resoluties GG en Raad, 18 March 1687.
5. ARA, VOC 702, fol. 209.
6. ARA, VOC 702, fols. 235, 254.
7. ARA, VOC 702, fol. 367.
8. ARA, VOC 702, fols. 254, 367, 381, and 410–413.
9. ARA, VOC 702, fol. 421.
10. ARA, VOC 702, fol. 429.
11. ARA, VOC 702, fol. 429.
12. ARA, VOC 702, fol. 596.
13. ARA, VOC 702, 29 August 1687.
14. ARA, VOC 702, 5 September 1687.
15. ARA, VOC 1431, fol. 769.
16. ARA, VOC 1431, fols. 766–771.
17. ARA, VOC 702, 21 November 1687.
18. ARA, VOC 702, unfoliated.
19. According to resolutions passed on 18 November, 28 November, and 2 December 1687, ARA, VOC 702.
20. ARA, VOC 702, 10 December 1687.

21. See Resoluties GG en Raad, 5 December 1687, ARA, VOC 702.

22. ARA, VOC 702.

23. J. W. Vogel, *Zehn-Jährige Ost-Indianische Reise-Beschreibung etc.* (Altenburg 1704), 498, 523.

24. Journal kept by Johan Bitter on the *Waalstroom*, NSM (I 176:XIV).

25. J. R. Bruijn, F. S. Gaastra, and I. Schöffer, *Dutch-Asiatic Shipping* (The Hague 1979), III, 127.

26. ARA, HR 783 fol. 100.

Notes to Chapter Ten
THE BITTER END

1. Motto recorded on the cover of the journal kept by Johan Bitter on the *Waalstroom*, NSM (I 176:XIV).

2. Van Alphen, *Papegaey*, II 327.

3. S. J. Fockema Andreae, *De Nederlandse staat onder de Republiek* (Amsterdam 1969), 142.

4. ARA, VOC 783, fol. 83.

5. ARA, VOC 783, fol. 91.

6. ARA, HR 783, fols. 84–91; ARA, HR 904.

7. ARA, VOC 783, fol. 92.

8. ARA, HR 783, fols. 93–95.

9. ARA, HR 904, 1 December 1691.

10. ARA, HR 904, 24 July 1692.

11. W. Wijnaendts van Resandt, *De gezaghebbers der Oost-Indische Compagnie op hare buitencomptoiren in Azië* (Amsterdam 1944).

12. L. Cortenraede, *De Wijkse regenten: van timmerman tot rentenier; Een prosopografisch onderzoek naar de regenten van Wijk bij Duurstede in het tweede stadhouderloze tijdperk* (Utrecht 1983).

13. RU, Archives of the Dutch Reformed Church, Wijk bij Duurstede, no. 176, accounts of the church warden, 1702–1715.

14. Cortenraede, *Wijkse regenten*, 105–107.

15. Ibid., 115.

16. RU, Archives of the Dutch Reformed Church, Wijk bij Duurstede, no. 176, accounts of the church warden, 1702–1715.

17. D. J. Roorda, "Het onderzoek naar het stedelijk patriciaat in Nederland" in W. W. Mijnhardt (ed.), *Kantelend geschiedbeeld* (Utrecht 1983), 124.

18. L. Cortenraede, *Wijkse regenten*, 54–55.

19. See RU, States of Utrecht, no. 217–364.

20. For the marriage certificate of 14 January 1704, see RU, notarial archives Van Sandick (Wijk bij Duurstede), Wij 008 a 009.

21. For the marriage certificate see RU, Van Boetzelaer family archives, no. 484, marriage settlement of Albert Jan van Lidth de Jeude and Aletta Bitter, 1707.

22. Arnolt arrived in Batavia in 1703, where he was given a seat on the Court of Justice. In 1705 he was transferred to Malabar in the capacity of deputy commander and administrator. In the General Missive of 25 November 1708 he is recorded as having been promoted to the post of *Advocaat-fiscaal* (Attorney General). He returned to Holland as vice-admiral of the autumn fleet of 1715; Coolhaas, *Generale Missiven*, VII, 166.

23. Johan and Dirk Nobel were sent to Holland in 1696 and 1699, respectively. See K. L. van Schouwenburg, "Over de Nobels; Genealogie en geschiedenis" in *De Nederlandse leeuw*, 103 (1986), 23.

24. RU, Van Boetzelaer family archives, no. 483.

25. See, for instance, RU, notarial archives Van Sandick, Wij 008 a 004, 1697: Bitter received 1,200 guilders + 4% interest from Batavia; Wij 008 a 010, 1707: Bitter received 300 guiders in bills of exchange from Batavia and 2,570 guilders in salary earned by Arnolt Bitter.

26. Van Schouwenburg, "Over de Nobels," 18–21. Bitter paid back the entire amount before his death in 1714.

27. RU, notarial archives Nicolaes Keppel, Wij 007 a 001: 30 July 1698. He used his position as proxy to collect his son's earnings.

28. GA, Weeskamer (Orphans' Chamber), "Register of guardianships beginning 21 October 1687 and ending 9 August 1707," nos. 5073–5518; GA Weeskamer, "Inbreng register," vol. 38, fol. 31.

29. RU, Wij 008 a 002, notarial archives Van Sandick, 1694.

30. GA, notarial archives Daniël Moors, 247–6318, 1693–1719, p. 829, "Last will of Jonker Jacobus Wijbrandt Cnoll, executed on 23 August 1702."

Notes to the Afterword

1. As Richard Holmes so nicely put it in "In de voetsporen van de biograaf" (In the footsteps of the biographer), Machteld Allen and René Moerland (eds.), *Gesprekken met tijdreizigers*, Amsterdam UP, 1993, 147.

2. *Alle de Wercken van den Heere Jacob Cats*, Amsterdam 1712.

3. Taylor, Jean Gelman, *The Social World of Batavia. European and Eurasian in Dutch Asia*, Madison, Wisconsin 1983.

4. Fockema Andreae, *De Nederlandse Staat*, 80.

5. Van Deursen, *Kopergeld*, III, 14–23.

6. D. J. Roorda, *Partij en factie* (Groningen 1978), 49.

7. J. S. Mill, *The Subjection of Women* (Cambridge, Mass. 1981), 31.

8. L. Bonfield, *Marriage Settlements, 1601–1740* (Cambridge 1983). For a picture of divorce cases in early-modern England, see Lawrence Stone, *Family, Sex and Marriage in England 1500–1800* (New York 1977).

9. Blijf, wat ge waart, toen ge blonkt als een bloem: / Zorg, dat Europa den zetel der orde, / Dat de verdrukte zijn wijkplaats U noem, / Land mijner Vad'ren mijn lust en mijn roem! Written by E. J. Potgieter in 1832 and published in 1833 in the periodical *Vaderlandsche Letteroefeningen*.

Suggested Reading

There is an enormous amount of literature on colonial Batavia and modern Jakarta, as witnessed by the 5,372 entries in *Batavia-Jakarta, 1600-2000, A Bibliography*, compiled by E. Ebing and Y. de Jager, Leiden: KITLV Press, 2000. Most of this literature is in Dutch and Indonesian, however, and very hard to come by in the English-speaking world. The only work in Dutch I mention here is the *magnum opus* by F. de Haan, *Oud Batavia*, Bandoeng: Nix Publishers, 1935. All historians of Batavia are indebted to this treasure trove, which also contains magnificent illustrations.

The following titles should be available in American bookstores and libraries.

An informative introduction to the general history of the city is given by Susan Abeyasekere in *Jakarta: A History*, Oxford: Oxford University Press, 1987.

Various aspects of Batavia's history are highlighted in a conference volume edited by Kees Grijns and Peter J.M. Nas, *Jakarta-Batavia*, Leiden: KITLV Press, 2001.

A useful guide for those interested in visiting the historical sites is A. Heuken, *Historical Sites of Jakarta*, second edition, Jakarta: Cipta Loka Caraka Publishers, 1983.

The best social history written in English of Batavia's colonial society is Jean Gelman Taylor, *The Social World of Batavia: European and Eurasian in Dutch Asia*, Madison: University of Wisconsin Press, 1983.

The position of mestizo women in Batavia is elucidated in Leonard Blussé, *Strange Company: Chinese settlers, mestizo women and the Dutch in* VOC *Batavia,* Leiden: KITLV Press, 1986.

Available through the UMI Dissertation Services is the unpublished dissertation by Pamela Anne McVay on the criminal justice system in Batavia, *I Am the Devil's Own: Crime, Class and Identity in the Seventeenth Century Dutch East Indies,* University of Illinois at Urbana-Champaign, 1995.

For a comparison with the position of women in other colonial societies, see C. R. Boxer, *Mary and Misogyny: Women in Iberian expansion overseas, 1415-1815. Some facts, fancies and personalities,* London: Duckworth Publishers, 1975; Teotonio R. de Souza, *Medieval Goa,* New Delhi: Concept Publishers, 1979; and finally, although it deals with a somewhat later period, Kenneth Ballhatchet, *Race, Sex and Class under the Raj: Imperial Attitudes and Policies and their Critics, 1793-1905,* New Delhi: Vikas Publishers, 1979.

For an introduction to the colonial world of the Dutch East India Company, see George Masselman, *The Cradle of Colonialism,* New Haven: Yale University Press, 1963, which deals with the earliest period, and the masterly overview by C.R. Boxer, *The Dutch Seaborne Empire, 1600-1800,* Harmondsworth: Penguin Books, 1973.

Simon Schama has written a challenging analysis of social life in the Dutch republic, *The Embarrassment of Riches: An Interpretation of Dutch Culture in the Golden Age,* London: William Collins, 1987.

The standard work on early-modern Dutch society remains Jonathan Israel's all-encompassing study, *The Dutch Republic: Its Rise, Greatness, and Fall, 1477-1806,* Oxford: Clarendon Press, 1995.

About the Author, Translator and Illustrator

LEONARD BLUSSÉ studied sinology, anthropology, and history at the universities of Leiden, Taipei, and Kyoto, and acquired his Ph.D. in history from Leiden University. He now occupies the chair of Asian-European Relations at Leiden University and also teaches Southeast Asian History at Xiamen University, China. Over the years he has spent his sabbaticals doing research in Tokyo, NIAS/Wassenaar, and the Davis Center at Princeton University. In 2005–2006 he will teach history at Harvard University.

Blussé's wide-ranging interests in the history of European expansion and global interaction have led him to publish works on topics from Chinese and Southeast Asian history to biographies to general histories of East-West relations. He has written or (co-) edited dozens of books, which have been translated into languages including Chinese, English, German, and Indonesian, as well as many academic articles. His books include *Companies and Trade: Essays on Overseas Trading Companies during the Ancien Regime*; *Strange Company: Chinese Settlers, Mestizo Women and the Dutch in VOC Batavia*; *Zhong-he jiaowang shi* (A History of Sino-Dutch Relations); *Pilgrims to the Past: Private Conversations with Historians of European Expansion*; *On the Eighteenth Century as a Category of Asian History: Van Leur in Retrospect*; *Bridging the Divide: 400 years of Dutch-Japanese Relations*; and *Shiba shiji-mo Badaweiya Tangrenshihui* (The Chinese Community of Batavia at the End of the Eighteenth Century).

In addition to having supervised many doctoral dissertations, Blussé, who wishes to be seen primarily as an educator, now heads the TANAP (Towards a New Age of Partnership) program, a large international cooperation project aimed at training young Asian historians in the early modern history of Asian trade and society.

DIANE WEBB, a professional musician and translator, lives in the Netherlands and Italy. She has translated the work of major Dutch writers in the fields of history and art history, including two books by Herman Pleij (*Dreaming of Cockaigne* and *Colors Demonic and Divine*) for Columbia University Press, Willem van Kemenade's *China, Hong Kong, Taiwan, Inc.* for Knopf, and *The European Colonial Empires 1815–1919* by H. L. Wesseling for Peason/Longman. Her translation of Maarten Prak's *Golden Age* will be published by Cambridge University Press in 2005.

Her translations of essays have appeared in the catalogues of numerous major museums, including the Metropolitan Museum of Art (New York), The Fine Arts Museums of San Francisco, The High Museum of Art (Atlanta), The National Gallery of Scotland, the Kröller-Müller Museum, and the Rijksmuseum and the Van Gogh Museum (Amsterdam). She is currently part of the team of five translators selected to translate the complete letters of Vincent van Gogh, a project sponsored by the Van Gogh Museum. The publication is scheduled to appear in 2008.

MARIA MADONNA DAVIDOFF studied fine arts at the University of the Philippines and works as a book designer and painter. She has exhibited her paintings and scrolls in galleries in Europe, Asia, and North America, including shows in Manila, New Delhi, Toronto, Washington, San Diego, Tokyo, and New York. Her museum exhibits include the Musée d'art et d'histoire de Fribourg, Switzerland, the Museum of Natural History, New York, the GSIS Museum Manila, and in 2005 the Vargas Museum in Manila.